forever beautiful with rex

forever beautiful with rex

beauty strategies for the rest of your life

written by diana lewis jewell
illustrations by rex

photographs by peter sakas and donald penny

Clarkson Potter/Publishers
New York

Published by Clarkson N. Potter, Inc., 201 East 50th
Street, New York, New York 10022. Member of the
Crown Publishing Group.

Random House, Inc. New York, Toronto, London,
Sydney, Auckland

CLARKSON N. POTTER, POTTER and colophon are
trademarks of Clarkson N. Potter, Inc.

Manufactured in Hong Kong
Designed by Richard Ferretti

Library of Congress Cataloging-in-Publication Data
Jewell, Diana Lewis.
    Forever beautiful with Rex : beauty strategies for
the rest of your life / written by Diana Lewis Jewell. —
1st ed.
            p.   cm.
    1. Beauty, Personal. 2. Middle aged women.
3. Cosmetics. I. Rex. II. Title.
RA778.J55 1994
646.7'042—dc20   93-124
                                        CIP

ISBN 0-517-58241-4
10 9 8 7 6 5 4 3 2 1
First edition

c o n t e n t s

Acknowledgments

Being forever beautiful involves much more than the artful application of makeup. Although that is Rex's area of expertise, we had to turn to many other experts in the beauty and health fields for the in-depth information that must accompany any study of the aging process.

We wish to thank, for their time, guidance, and considerable help, the following people:

Dr. Michael Evan Sachs, director of research and associate professor of Facial Plastic and Reconstructive Surgery at the New York Eye and Ear Infirmary, New York Medical College. As an inventor-surgeon, Dr. Sachs has innovated several new plastic surgery procedures, including finesse sculpting rhinoplasty, cartilage glues, tissue clay, and fat-melting blepharoplasty. In addition, Dr. Sachs has pioneered many new techniques in facial reconstruction after paralysis, cancer surgery, and trauma. He has published over forty research papers and a series of reference textbooks. He has been actively teaching facial plastic surgery for over a decade, and is one of the elite group of surgeons who writes the exam for board certification in Facial Plastic and Reconstructive Surgery.

Dr. John R. Anton, chief of plastic surgery at Southampton Hospital. After serving a residency in general surgery on the Harvard Surgical Service at New England Deaconess Hospital and at the Massachusetts General Hospital in Boston, Dr. Anton then served a fellowship in Plastic and Reconstructive Surgery at Wayne State University. Today, he specializes in all aspects of plastic and reconstructive surgery, including burn treatment, hand surgery, and all aesthetic procedures for the face and body.

Dr. Michael Bruce Klein, D.D.S., P.C. provided in-depth "tutorials" on the aging process of the teeth, mouth, and gums, as well as information on modern corrective procedures.

For their considerable knowledge of the "stuff" cosmetics are made of, we wish to thank Linda Katana and Harvey Kornhaber for their help.

John Frommer, the guru of hair color for celebrities such as Candice Bergen, Liza Minnelli, Yoko Ono, and many other notable personalities, explained just what can and can't be done for beautifying the hair as one gets older.

Peter Sakas and Donald Penny have photographed the most beautiful models in the business, and our "real women" are no exception. Our thanks to them both for their studios, skill, and beautiful pictures. Jim Crawford and Andrew Di Simone also turned heads with their hairstyling magic at each session. We thank you, and the women who were photographed for this book thank you.

Which leads us to the wonderful women who were beautiful before, during, and after the shoot. Some are clients, some are in the business of beauty themselves. Thanks to all of you for consenting to be a part of this book, and for showing us how wonderful a woman can look—at any age! Karen Sakas, Carlotta Jacobson, Ella May Lewis, Jane Chang, Patti Cohen, Audrey Schmaltz, Sally Harlor, Annchen Kitchener, Cecile Engle, Donna Lang, Elisa Priano, and Suzanne Hastings.

Finally, as ever, we wish to thank our agent, Connie Clausen, for insisting that this book be done—and that we should be the ones to do it—and our very astute editor, Pam Krauss, who grows more beautiful with every passing book!

Rex Hilverdink and Diana Lewis Jewell

Introduction

So when did it start? Were those "tiny dry lines" cosmetic companies are so quick to warn us about the first signs that the character of your beauty was about to change? Or did you notice nothing in the mirror but, suddenly, everything in a photograph? Could those extra pouches under your chin really be yours? And where did that network of lines come from? It's sometimes painful and it's often startling to see yourself the way others see you, and not the reflection in your favorite makeup mirror.

There are many ways to discover that your skin is beginning to feel its age, and I think each one comes as a surprise. The first time you find the imprints of your fingers in your cheek after leaning your face on your hand. The first time under-eye puffiness doesn't completley disappear—even after you're up and about. The first time you sweep eye shadow across your lid, and the skin stretches out, but not back. Little by little, these experiences tell you something. And they're much more revealing than finding that first wrinkle. Wrinkles, we expect. Loss of elasticity and tone seem a lot more frightening.

In the end, of course, it doesn't really matter when the first signs of aging appear. Because they start before you notice it. You're not looking for clues in your late twenties. But after twenty-six the skin's regenerative powers start slowing down. Underneath the surface, your skin's support system is changing, and sooner or later the change is going to show. In Chapter One, I'll explain just what changes the appearance and the performance of your skin as you get older, just so you know (and just so you realize that some of the more remarkable "anti-aging" creams really can't do a thing about it). Of course, there are ways to treat skin during the natural process of aging to make it look its radiant best, but to date, no one has discovered a way to reverse the process itself. So we must learn to live with these changes, and do what we can to make them less apparent.

That's why this book really isn't about aging. It's about being beautiful, year after year. After all, you've got more of these years left after the "bloom" of youth has passed than before. You shouldn't feel as if you're on the "wrong side" of beautiful for most of your life; every age, every stage of life you go through, has its own unique beauty. You simply have to learn how to capture it.

As time goes by, you may find you need to make some changes in your beauty and makeup routine; to reassess your particular strengths and trouble spots. But just as your skin is changing, so should your total image evolve to express the woman you've become, not the girl you've left behind.

I'm not going to tell you how to look younger. Why? Because true beauty is a process of becoming. In all of nature, beauty is a gradual unfolding, not the quicksilver flash of youth. What I am going to tell you is how to take what you've got—good and bad—and make the best of it. And that's all you really need to do— at any age.

000 Rexx

the physiology of aging

what's changing
. . . and why

chapter 1

"You're not getting older, you're getting better." This wonderful advertising slogan from a few years ago helped to change the perception of the maturing woman. Soon entire magazines were created for women who had gotten beyond girlhood, and were proud of it. Cosmetic companies devoted substantial research and development budgets to products formulated especially for the unique characteristics of aging skin. So why do women still regard each passing birthday with dread? You are changing, no doubt about it. You're a different woman than you were at twenty, or even thirty, but that's not necessarily a negative thing. Look at it this way: You have all of your life experiences to bring to your smile, your charm, your beauty. You have a much better knowledge of what works for you, and what doesn't. You're not going to experiment with every crazy color trend that comes along. Tangerine eyelids, fuchsia lips? Fine, but not for you. You have a sense of who you are, what you look like, how you want to be perceived, and that confidence comes through. So it's really a new you, not an aging you, that you are now becoming acquainted with. And the adventure of discovery can be very exciting.

I wish I could say you are undergoing a physiological metamorphosis as beneficial as your psychological metamorphosis, but the truth is, certain things are weakening. It happens to everybody along the way, and it's helpful to understand just what is going on inside and outside the body. A wrinkle isn't put there to punish you because you smiled too much, or used your face too expressively. Normal facial motion has nothing to do with the creation of wrinkles. But your skin, and its evolution, does. So that is where we will start.

Skin Deep

The Basic Facts

The skin is a marvelous machine. It doesn't simply exist, covering your body like an invisible shield. It is a vital, functioning system that keeps you waterproof, airtight, and flexible. It maintains body temperature, no matter what's going on around you. It keeps fluids in, bacteria out. And it is your first line of defense against life-threatening disease.

Your skin is your body's biggest organ, the largest one of your body, and it is intimately involved in all life processes. Just under the surface of the skin, the essential interchange of absorption, circulation, and elimination goes on, producing the energy needed for growth and maintenance. Millions of new red blood cells are produced every minute. Tissues are repaired and replenished. Food particles are chemically broken down and moved across cell membranes. Biochemical cellular activity gives us warmth, energy, life.

Continual cellular and tissue regeneration determines the health and vitality of the skin. Indeed, the surface of the skin itself is nothing more than an accumulation of dead cells that have been pushed up, ready for shedding. If allowed to accumulate excessively, these cells can give skin a dull, lifeless appearance and they can also block pores, preventing emollients from reaching the part of the skin that needs them most! Using a mild exfoliant two or three times a week will slough off dead cells and bring back the glow to your skin.

This top layer of the epidermis, or stratum corneum, is the major physical barrier to the environment. In fact, the protein material that makes it up, keratin, is especially effective in absorbing harmful ultraviolet rays before they penetrate the skin's surface. So you must treat the skin that faces up to the world with care. Keep it well-cleansed, free of ashy buildup, and lubricated with a light moisturizer.

Just beneath the epidermis is the dermis, the skin layer most affected by the aging process. It is here that the fibrous "support system" of the skin, the collagen and elastin, is housed. This network of interlocking protein fibers makes the skin firm and resilient. Collagen is the most abundant protein in the body, found in the skin and all connective tissues. It is the basic "glue" that binds the cells together. As we age, it becomes increasingly rigid and inflexible. (In fact, the conversion ratio of soluble to insoluble collagen is a very accurate indicator of chronological age.)

Signs of Change

Molecular biologists have now identified a group of genes that trigger aging in skin cells, blood vessel cells, and some brain cells, paving the way for the development of compounds that may reverse the whole process. The possibility of eliminating wrinkles and restoring the texture of aging skin may well be what the future holds!

In the meantime, though, we have to face up to our faces! And to understand just what's going on, it is best to know how and why skin begins to show its age.

The collapsing of collagen is what contributes to the wrinkling and sagging of the skin. If you think of these fibers as the framework within your skin, you can understand what happens when this supporting structure falls down. The dermis literally caves in. When you see this effect on the surface of the skin, there's no mistaking it: It's a wrinkle.

Wrinkle patterns can be inherited, but the extent of the wrinkling has more to do with your lifestyle, your unprotected exposure to the elements, and your general health. Great-Grandma may actually have had fewer wrinkles than you do at her age today, but then, maybe she didn't jog, garden, or play golf!

Of course, wrinkling isn't all that happens to skin as it ages. Epidermal cell generation slows, decreasing by almost 50 percent postmenopause, and the skin becomes thinner and less flexible. It is less able to repair damaged cells, and less capable of retaining its critical moisture level. To make matters worse, the sebaceous glands, those wonderful oil dischargers that may have been working overtime during adolescence, begin cutting back as estrogen and progesterone levels drop. The natural skin oil they produce, which is actually a complex mix of fats and waxes, serves to coat the skin and "lock in" its natural moisture. With a diminished amount of these natural oils, skin becomes dry and rough, making wrinkles even more apparent.

Sebaceous glands lie to the side of hair follicles, oil's avenue to the surface. This brings us to the third layer of skin structure: the subcutaneous tissue. Hair follicles are either deep in the dermis, or in the subcutaneous tissue, the fatty "shock absorber" that acts as the body's insulator and helps maintain its temperature. Subcutaneous tissue also thins with age, particularly in the face and hands. Skin loses its "cushiony" feeling and becomes more sensitive to cold, more susceptible to injury. At this point, skin is at its most vulnerable, and may be prone to dermatitis and environmental damage. Some areas may become as thin as parchment.

These are the physiological changes that account for the normal appearance of aging. Photoaging is what the sun does to your skin, and is even worse because it accelerates the entire process. In fact, sun exposure is responsible for 80 percent of the visible signs of aging!

Sun...Your Skin's Worst Enemy

Generations ago, when a suntan was considered a sign of coarseness, women used to shield their delicate skin from sun exposure with parasols, wide-brimmed hats, gloves, and long, flowing skirts. They had the right idea. Unfortunately, suntans changed their status over the past seventy-some years and became associated with luxury and leisure.

Today, any dermatologist will tell you a suntan is simply a sign of ignorance. First of all, beyond any cosmetic considerations, the sun is dangerous to your health. Plain and simple, it encourages the formation of cancer cells. If sunshine were packaged and commercially sold, it would have to bear a warning from the Surgeon General! The American Cancer Society reports well over five hundred thousand cases of skin cancer a year, and in some cases it is fatal. The incidence of malignant melanoma, the deadliest form of skin cancer, is increasing faster than any other type of cancer. As the sun-blocking ozone layer continues to deteriorate, things are only going to get worse.

Fortunately, Mother Nature provides us with some defense against the sun, right in our own skin. The protein, keratin, is highly efficient in absorbing ultraviolet (UV) rays. Other cells in the epidermis, known as melanocytes, produce melanin, another defense weapon in the body's anti-cancer arsenal. These pigment cells help block ultraviolet penetration. In fact, the darker pigmentation of a suntan shows these cells at work. Tanning is simply the skin's reaction to injury from ultraviolet light.

There are two dangerous wavelengths in the UV spectrum that you currently must shield skin against at all times. They are the UVA and UVB rays. The most dangerous, UVB, causes sunburn, wrinkles, and skin cancer. At temperate latitudes, it penetrates the atmosphere most between about 10:00 A.M. and 3:00 P.M. Ultraviolet A beams through all day, and can do plenty of damage in its own right. In summer sunlight, there may be as much as a thousand times more UVA than UVB. It contributes to the photoaging of the skin, causes sunburn, and is also implicated in skin cancer. Since your skin is constantly being bombarded with UVA rays, no matter what the season, no matter what the weather, it makes sense to protect against them, as well.

A third UV wavelength, identified as C, is potentially the most hazardous. Not much of it is getting through to us presently, but with ozone atmosphere depletion, it may become our worst enemy of all!

The effects of sun exposure are cumulative over the years, and they are, to a great extent, irreversible. The frightening fact is, as much as 80 percent of the damage occurs before the age of twenty! Avoiding sun exposure as a child is the best way to prevent the appearance of premature aging in the adult years. But, sadly, once the damage is done, it's done. Sun exposure breaks down the fatty layer, as well as the elastin cells and collagen within the dermis; it deepens wrinkles into furrows, gives skin a tough, leathery texture, explodes tiny red "spider" veins all over, and discolors and mottles skin with uneven pigmentation. What you might be calling "age" spots or "liver" spots, I call sunspots, because they're the result of years of sun damage. Ultraviolet rays can cause erratic pigmentation of the skin on the face, arms, and hands, just as the hormonal changes that come with aging can make skin blotchy. It's a one-two combination punch that can make you look splotchy, spotty, and just plain old.

If skin remained undamaged by the sun, many visible signs of aging would never appear, and those that did would be less severe. Although the changes happen gradually (it can take up to twenty-five years for collagen and elastin damage to be significant enough to show on the surface as wrinkles and sagging), cellular damage cannot be reversed by daily moisturizing. However, protecting your skin from the sun does allow for actual repair of damaged skin and the generation of new collagen and elastin fibers.

No one is immune from the effects of UV radiation, although fair-skinned people, who naturally have thinner skin, are far more vulnerable to damage; fine lines and internal deterioration can start at an earlier age. Those with medium to darker complexions can count their lucky stars because they'll count fewer wrinkles! However, the deeper they tan, the more extensive the skin damage.

There's absolutely no safety in tanning machines, either. Tanning booths emit higher UVA and UVB intensities than the hottest summer sun. Even do-it-yourself sunlamps are dangerous. The FDA permits as much as 5 percent of UVB light in these appliances (although UVB in sunlight is only 1 percent), and the UVA emission is one hundred times that found in natural sunlight. So "instant" sun is instant trouble!

In addition to the skin damage caused by UV radiation, the sun sets up a chemical reaction with the oxygen in the air, causing the formation of free radicals, charged particles that damage cell walls like rust on a car. These tireless scavengers launch thousands of attacks on every human cell each day.

No one can escape the fact that age brings changes to skin texture and tone, but going into the sun unprotected is like going into a time machine set on fast-forward! The best anti-wrinkle cream I know is a good sunblock, with an SPF of 15 or higher, liberally applied. And this should begin from Day One to reduce the effects of lifetime sun damage. Although do keep in mind that SPF protection is not a "free pass" to day-long sunning. There simply is *no* safe way to tan.

On the Surface of Things . . . Structure Changes, Too

Y ou know the familiar map of your face. You've been over it thousands of times. Yet although all change is gradual, structural changes always seem to come like a thief in the night. One day you have a strong, firm chin line, the next day there is a hint of a jowl. One day you have a definite demarcation in the crease of your eyelid, the next day it seems to be puffy from brow to lash.

Nature pulls all lines down as we age; there's no mystery to the direction they're going to go. But wrinkling patterns do vary from person to person. Some of it depends on heredity, some depends on the degree of sun and environmental exposure, and some depends on face-changing habits like smoking. A "smoker's mouth" is very easy to spot. It is characterized by deeper puckers all around the lips, in addition to tooth discoloration. Squint lines at the corners of the eyes can also become exaggerated. Think of the grimace many smokers make as they inhale, and you'll see that this habit only accentuates the negative. Not only is smoking hazardous to your health (and, very likely, to those

around you), it's disastrous to your beauty!

Your own personal pattern of lines, creases, folds, and pouches may favor one part of your face more than another. Many women with severe crepiness at the neck and jawline have perfectly smooth foreheads. Women with deeply furrowed tension lines between the brows may have very light lining at the sides of the mouth. And women with a multitude of "crow's feet" crinkles may have an otherwise youthful complexion. Of course, you can also have a soupçon of everything! In truth, most people do, but aging is often more pronounced in one area than another.

When do these harbingers of your "future" face first appear? They actually begin in the mid-to-late twenties. And the eyes are always the first to show it. That's because the skin there, especially on the upper lids, is thinner than anyplace else in the body. It also has fewer oil glands to keep it moist and young-looking. Chances are, you'll notice the resiliency of the skin beginning to give way as you apply your eye shadow (constant stretching of the skin doesn't help the situation—be gentle with all applicators!).

Underneath the eye is another telltale region, although it shows signs of deterioration a bit later than the upper lids. Morning under-eye puffiness has to do with hydrostatic pressure. All that means is, the water gravitates to that area when you're stationary. Get going, and the edema recedes. Until one day it doesn't.

The tissue under your eyes is extremely thin and delicate; it stretches easily to accommodate fat and fluids. As the ligament that normally supports this protective layer of under-eye fat weakens, the skin begins to sag. Sagging skin and protruding fat cause shadows, which show up as dark "circles" under the eyes. Typically, this occurs in the forties, although bags and dark circles may show up in the mid-thirties, or earlier if inherited. Hormonal changes, which contribute to water retention, also aid and abet under-eye pouching. The skin there is a willing reservoir!

Men are less susceptible to these structural signs of aging. Aging around the eyes begins about a decade later for them because their underlying ligaments are stronger, and their skin is 10 to 15 percent thicker, so it resists stretching. They also don't pull and push the skin every day applying and removing makeup—but I'm not about to suggest you stop wearing it!

As the map of your face changes, you simply have to approach makeup application differently. Learn the new topography; don't be afraid of it. It's friendly territory. After all, it's you. But it's not the same you. The angles have changed and softened; the distance from one feature to another may have changed; the height and width of the mouth also may have changed; possibly, too, the length of the nose. So the old rules don't apply, can't apply. Putting your makeup on the same way you have since you were twenty years old is like putting on someone else's makeup. The illusion of beauty has much to do with maintaining proper proportion and balance. If you don't pay attention to the new structure of your face, you'll find that you're off kilter.

So, take a good, long look in a strong, bright light. Clear your skin of all makeup and leave only the lightest glow of a very sheer moisturizer. This will help reflect the light so you can see the shape and structure better. Sweep your hair back with a band to determine your actual face shape. Don't automatically assume that it's *still* long and narrow, or a perfect oval. Since when? Slight jowling (which can happen anytime after thirty) may have squared off your narrow face; a little extra under the chin may have rounded off your oval.

What we're dealing with now, from this moment on, is the face you have today. The one that's going to be even *more* beautiful tomorrow! And the first lesson to learn is how to take the very best care of yourself . . . from the inside out!

the best beauty treatment

treatment

a commonsense approach

chapter 2

Somewhere along the way, you make your choice either to confront the signs of aging, head on, or ignore them. Many women choose the latter, under the guise of "growing old gracefully." Yet even if you opt to let nature take its course, there are simple, everyday, face-saving things you can do to maintain the beauty of your skin. So why not do them?

Some women, and maybe you're one of them, are too busy, or too impatient, or too suspicious of outward shows of vanity. They don't even notice they're getting older, and they're actually not very concerned about any change in their appearance. They wear minimal makeup, if any, and probably always have. Theirs is not the art of deception, theirs is the badge of acceptance.

Those confident enough to let the chips fall where they may should still be concerned with keeping their skin fresh, soft, and glowing. But a soap-and-water splash just isn't going to do it. I don't care how simplified you want your beauty routine to be, the fact is, your skin is drying out, and it simply makes sense to use products designed to put moisture back, hold moisture in. I'll tell you the different types later in this chapter, and when and where to use them. But first let's consider the basics of beauty.

The Three Faces of Beauty

Look in the mirror and what do you see? What's in a face besides the obvious configuration of bone structure and features? Appearance is actually a composite of three things: skin, complexion, and expression. Your skin is what you are, wrinkles and all. It is an impassive covering, an interchanging membrane that reacts immediately to any environment it's in. Your complexion is what gives you a glow, or robs you of years. This is where the care, or lack of it, really shows. And, finally, expression is what gives life to your features. It's what we remember of someone's face. A smile is 75 percent of your image. We don't see the laugh lines, we see the smile. Lose it and frown . . . and all we see are wrinkles! A smile is the best way to improve your appearance instantly.

We're as good on the outside as we are on the inside. It's really that simple. The condition of your skin gives everything away: your age, your health, your emotions, your habits. It can tell the world if you've been staying up too late, if you smoke, if you're under stress, if you're not exercising. The skin keeps no secrets. Why? Some telltales are purely a function of body chemistry. If you smoke, for instance, you inhibit the oxygen supply in the skin and interfere with its capillary circulation, which, in turn, damages the surface tissue. If you've got a toxic buildup (too much alcohol, stress, the wrong foods), you're contributing to the formation of free radicals in the cells (those very destructive particles I discussed in the last chapter). If you're tired or sick, skin tone may turn slightly gray or yellow because of circulatory sluggishness, quite the opposite from the tone it takes on when you've been pumping your blood around with exercise. It is well documented that bone becomes less dense with inertia, so there is a distinct possibility that the same thing may happen with the collagen of the skin. If you don't stay active, your muscles aren't the only thing that will be out of shape! The best beauty tip I or anyone can give you is to eat well, sleep well, and maintain regularity well. Because it's going to show.

In addition to the basic biological reactions affecting beauty, the way you look clearly demonstrates the care you take of your face—and your body. That's why I always tell women to treat themselves very kindly, with a regular system of personal *and* professional care. It always surprises me when a woman follows better maintenance procedures for her nails, her wardrobe, her car, than she does for the beginning—and end—of all beauty: her skin. If you want it to pass its 15,000-, 20,000- and 25,000-day checkup with flying colors, you had better keep it well tuned every single day.

Here are a few things you can do to make sure your skin is operating at peak efficiency. There are everyday musts, weekly treats, and emergency measures, and a good skin-care regimen always includes a little of each.

Be Very Stimulating

Skin thrives on stimulation and there's a very good reason. Massage can actually stimulate blood flow and improve the skin's appearance. As a bonus, it also helps slough away the surface layer of dry, dulling dead skin cells. Your skin is choking beneath them, blocked from the rejuvenating effects of oxygen and emollients.

Nothing replaces a professional exfoliation performed in a skin-care salon. A mask or scrub done by expert hands leaves skin soft, smooth, and glowing. Once a month isn't too often to schedule such a treatment, if you continue to supplement this care with milder treatment masks one to three times a week at home. How often you do it depends on your skin type and response.

In general, dry, moisture-starved skin needs a mask that doesn't strip away essential oils, or disturb the mineral equilibrium of the skin. A mask as creamy as a moisturizer that tissues off, rather than peels off, is best. Oil-clogged skin benefits

from masks containing a form of clay or mud. These very absorbent ingredients are particularly effective in removing impurities as they blot up excess oil. Mineral-enriched clay masks are best, as drying skin out tends to remove minerals which must be replenished to maintain the balance of surface electrolytes. Many mud masks now contain sea vegetables, a highly concentrated source of minerals as well as trace elements in their balanced state. Seaweed also supplies alginic acid, which has an elasticizing effect as it dilates the capillaries, improving circulation. All of these are of benefit to sluggish, oily skin.

Even normal skin improves in texture and tone with regular mask treatment. Gels that stiffen and peel off can refine and hydrate the skin, tightening pores and diminishing dry lines. No mask will "unwrinkle" you, but the temporary refreshment is like sending your face to a spa.

Whenever your skin begins to look a little lifeless, use a mask to stimulate the circulation and cleanse the skin. You'll be able to tell just how often your skin needs this extra energy boost, but keep in mind that three applications a week isn't overdoing it for the driest skin.

As you apply any mask or cream, always use upward strokes, beginning at the base of your throat. Why contribute to the downward pull of gravity? Use light, fingertip pressure; never pull or drag your skin. Around the eye area, press gently in small circles, from the bridge of the nose outward and along and over the orbital bone. This relaxes the tension and relieves the pressure caused by sinus congestion and water retention. Acupressure is a wonderful refreshment for the face, and it does much more than isometric stretching. It's been proven that grimacing and relaxing or scowling and releasing actually has no effect when it comes to "toning" skin and muscles to eliminate sagging. However, certain stimulating gestures, done daily, can exercise and mobilize skin, improving circulation in the bargain. Just remember, be gentle and use a very light touch.

The Clean Routine
A Chance to Do Something Good for Your Skin Twice a Day

Starting every morning and ending every night with skin cleansed of all impurities, surface buildup, and airborne pollution is the best way I know to ensure skin longevity. In the morning, it is necessary to activate skin and eliminate stasis residue: oil buildup, night-cream film, dead skin cells. At night, it's absolutely essential to remove makeup and daily grime before your head hits the pillow. Left alone, oil and dirt can clog pores, resulting in the formation of pimples, cysts, blackheads . . . even acne! Yes, adult acne can and does occur, especially with hormonal changes. You're never too old for troubled skin.

A splash of water at the sink or in the shower is not going to do the job. Making your skin wet doesn't make it clean. That requires a surfactant— an agent that attracts both grease and water, binding them together so they can be rinsed away.

There are a variety of creams, lotions, cleansers, and soaps that contain these essential emulsifiers. The objective is to find the one that is *least* irritating to your skin. Before you make your selection, be aware that rinsing your skin with hard or highly chlorinated water can be devastatingly drying, no matter what type of cleansing agent you use.

Defined below are different types of cleansing products. It is wisest to select the type you want first, the brand name second.

Toilet Soaps Save them for the toilet! They're alkaline and can affect the skin's acid mantle. While they cleanse effectively, ridding skin of grime, grease, and residual buildup, they can be drying and irritating. Plus, they can form a sticky residue in hard water; leave it on your skin, and all is lost.

Moisturizing Soaps They start out as toilet soaps, and are supplemented with between 5 and 15 percent more fat, such as lanolin, oil, cocoa butter, and cold cream. Also called "superfatted soaps," these products tend to counteract the degreasing process as they moisturize the skin. While they're gentler and less drying than inexpensive toilet soaps, they can also leave a residue.

Transparent Soaps You should see right through the myth that they are any gentler for the skin than any other soap. Their glycerin and alcohol content can actually be drying or irritating to sensitive skin. If your skin is oily, however, this variety of superfatted soap may be just right for you.

Detergent Soaps Not as harsh as they sound, these synthetic soaps are less irritating and less alkaline than toilet soaps, and produce a rich lather. They don't react with hard water to leave a scummy film on your face, nor do they have such a high fat content that they leave a greasy residue.

Wash-Off Creams and Lotions Now we're getting into moisturizer territory. Cleansing agents are added to a moisturizer in its creamy state, or cleansing creams are thinned with water to make a lotion that rinses off with water. Dry or sensitive skin benefits most from this type of cleansing medium. If you don't feel clean unless your skin gets wet, these are perfect for you. They rinse off with water.

Wipe-Off Creams and Lotions Moisturizers, again, with mild cleansing properties, but these are richer and contain little or no detergent. Most effective for removing oil-based makeup, they are meant to be tissued off. Because they can leave a residue on the skin, be sure to follow up with a mild toner to remove all traces.

Toners and Astringents All fresheners contain some degree of alcohol to dissolve dirt and oils. Your skin will feel cool and refreshed when you use them, but the pore "tightening" actually comes from the irritation that causes pore openings to swell slightly, and is temporary, at best. Toners are effective for dissolving last traces of makeup, and

astringents do help to control excess oil between cleansings. However, dry or sensitive skin may be irritated by these tinglers.

Many cleansing products are sold as part of a cleanser/toner/moisturizer trilogy. The implication is you can't do one without the other. That's nonsense. Discuss your skin's temperament with beauty advisers behind the counter, and let them recommend a regimen formulated for your skin type. Then experiment. You may find that your skin thrives perfectly well with a two-step cleansing process . . . or even a simple moisturizing soap. Once your skin is perfectly clean, refreshed, and relaxed, it will accept a moisturizer that much better.

Moisturizers
The Best Thing You Can Do for Your Skin

Ask any woman which beauty enhancer she would most want with her if stranded on an island, and she'll probably name a makeup: a blusher, a mascara, a lipstick. A lot of good any of those are going to do when you skin is left defenseless against the sun. If you can have only one beautifier, opt for sunblock every time. If you can have two treasures, the next most important item for beauty maintenance is a moisturizer. You shouldn't spend a day without it.

Water is a natural component of healthy skin; the skin's outer layer is nearly 30 percent water, and water is one of the most important elements in determining skin's texture. With the progressive decline in skin hydration that is part of the aging process, cells begin to be shed in clumps, rather than individually. That's the flaking of dry skin. And it's a condition that affects everybody, sooner or later.

Dryness isn't just a simple loss of water from the skin, however. It gets more complicated than that. The outer layer can thicken or stiffen, resulting in greater evaporative water loss, which can eventually split and crack the hardened skin. Although this produces a fissure, not a wrinkle, it disturbs the smooth surface of the skin, accentuating wrinkles and robbing skin of its glow.

At the moment, nonprescriptive moisturizing creams do not affect the structure of the skin. But they *do* smooth and soften a surface damaged by dryness. Some of them, the ones known as humectants, actually draw moisture from the air and bind it to the skin. When combined with traditional moisturizing ingredients, such as animal, vegetable, or mineral oils, the higher the humectant concentration, the more effective the product is against severely dried skin.

The proportion of oil to water in a moisturizer is another indication of how well it's going to work for you. Water-based moisturizers (those containing more water than oil) may have been fine for you when your skin was a little more lubricated, but now they may be too light for you. Similarly, lotions, which are nothing more than creams to which water has been added, may not be as beneficial for your skin as a rich, oil-based cream. But try different formulations to find one that is right for you. If a cream feels suffocating, greasy, or sticky, don't even think about using it again.

And never, *ever* feel you must apply a moisturizer heavily for it to be effective. Actually, you should use only a small amount, or you'll trick your body into slowing down oil production—exactly the opposite of the effect you want!

What's in a Moisturizer?

It Helps to Speak the Language

The best moisturizers relieve dry surface conditions, provide long-lasting hydration, and protect the skin from daily environmental aggression. What a moisturizer does is supply moisture, or "hydration," to the upper layers of the skin, temporarily increasing its comfort level and flexibility. What it doesn't do is stimulate the oil glands to provide lubrication from within. But today's new technologies offer improved "delivery systems," ways of getting the moisturizer to the level of the stratum corneum, where it will do the most good. Below you'll find some of the language used to describe moisturizer formulations so you can choose one that is right for your skin.

Lipids Literally, the "mortar" of skin-cell layers, this is what fills in the spaces between cells, and prevents moisture loss. Man-made lipids called *ceramides* have been designed to help the skin retain its natural hydration, rather than supplying external hydration as traditional moisturizers would.

Silicones Oils that give a moisturizer better "slip" on the skin, imparting a silkiness, without a greasy feel. Found in moisturizers as well as some foundations, mascaras, and eye shadows.

Hyaluronic Acid An extremely effective humectant, naturally found in the skin's deeper layers. This ingredient pulls moisture from the air, as well as from deeper tissues, to the surface of the skin.

Liposomes Originally designed as a "delivery system" for drugs, these time-release ingredient containers carry moisturizing agents deeper into the skin's upper layers. The smaller the liposome, the more effectively it penetrates.

Microspheres Smaller liposomes made of lipids, which serves to bind the moisturizing ingredients within the skin.

Beauty as Easy as ABCDE

Many moisturizers and night creams contain vitamin derivatives. Antioxidants and vitamins C and E are often added to attack free radicals. Vitamin A is often claimed to deliver some of the benefits of retinoic acid. But results from the topical application of vitamins are hard to prove. The smarter place to put vitamins is in your diet. Optimum metabolic functioning means all systems are *go,* building and repairing—activities absolutely vital to the splendor of your skin. That's what's going to show up in your face.

vitamin A Maintains skin smoothness and elasticity; a good soldier against dry skin. Find it in liver, carrot juice, butter, fish, and whole milk.

vitamin B Purifies your complexion, contributing to a glossy, smooth glow. Have complete cereals and whole milk for breakfast, and you've got it.

vitamin C Helps build collagen and elastin fibers for firmer, younger-looking skin. Citrus fruit, Brussels sprouts, spinach, and parsley are all good sources.

vitamin D Essential for the growth and maintenance of strong bones. Sunlight helps our bodies synthesize our own Vitamin D, but if we block out UV rays, we must supply it in the diet. Fish liver oils and milk will provide it.

vitamin E Protects the cells by opposing oxidation and destruction, while it aids in transporting nourishment. Cold-pressed vegetable oils (sunflower, corn, or wheat germ), nuts, and raw seeds contain it.

Don't forget that proteins are very necessary to help cells synthesize collagen and elastin, your skin's structural support. They need the essential amino acids supplied by diet. So don't ignore eggs, milk, poultry, fish, and meat, while limiting intake of animal fats and total calories. Vegetables and fruits contain incomplete proteins and should be eaten with foods containing the amino acids they are missing. Otherwise, protein synthesis will slow down or stop. A protein deficiency shows up first in the hair, nails, skin, and muscle tone.

Take a Beauty Cocktail

Because nutrition is so closely connected with the glow of a healthy complexion, try a Spa Cleanse to clear the system—and the complexion. The restorative powers of a simplified, semi-liquid diet allows the digestive system to rest, while it flushes out toxins and excess water. Choose a day when you don't need peak energy (a Sunday, for example), and detox!

Start the day with a beauty cocktail: the juice of one-half grapefruit, one-half orange, and one lemon. Then flush the system and transport vitamins midmorning and midafternoon with your own special blend of vegetable juice, freshly made from two carrots, two sticks of celery, one apple, and parsley. As an alternative, "brew" a lemon tea. Add the juice of one lemon to a cup of hot water and float a slice or two on top. If you must sweeten, add just a bit of natural honey.

Rex's One-Day Spa Cleanse

Breakfast
Beauty cocktail

11:00 A.M.
Fresh vegetable juice or hot water with lemon

Lunch
Two cups of degreased bouillon, with a dash of freshly squeezed lemon

4:00 P.M.
Fresh vegetable juice or hot water with lemon

Dinner
5 ounces of grilled or steamed fish fillets or 1 cup of cottage cheese with yogurt and mint tea

Before Bed
Hot-water lemon "tea" with one teaspoon of honey

Sweet Dreams
A Healing Time for Your Skin

The work of your body goes on at night, even while you are resting. It's a time for skin to recover from the assault of the day: Sunlight, pollution, sweat, heating systems, air conditioning, you name it, your face has had to fight it. And, at night, it has to address the damage.

Growth hormone is secreted during sleep, which may affect skin-growth factors. Cells may replicate faster, and certain enzymes in the body may be more active at night. Most important, however, the daily level of environmental irritation is removed: your skin isn't facing the traumatic negative reactions that stress skin (UV rays, pollution, smoke) all day.

You can give your skin a head start on its nightly restorative function by removing every external trace of grime and oil. Then moisturize lightly with a good night cream. You want to clean, soothe, and relax your skin so it can refresh and re-energize itself while you sleep.

Do Night Creams Really Help Repair Skin?

Although there are ingredients that will hasten the normal process of shedding, allowing fresh cells to rise to the surface, no night cream has been formulated that will actually speed cell regeneration. But that doesn't mean you should send your skin to bed without any supper! Think of a night cream as a nourishing energizer that gives your skin a better glow, a smoother surface, and a revitalized finish by day. Your makeup will look the prettier for it.

There are many restorative treatments on the market developed to soothe and settle the skin without the irritating ingredients used to shield skin by day. Sunscreens, for instance, serve no purpose in a nightly moisturizer. Many add calming botanical ingredients, essential oils from plants and herbs, to soothe skin. On the whole, night creams are lighter, less draggy than they used to be, so they won't just "sit" on the skin and plump it all out of proportion. Some are gel-based, while others are very sheer liquids, formulated with humectants, to provide maximum hydration. You don't need a lot, and you don't need to worry about morning eye puffiness, if it is properly applied. Simply don't apply a night cream closer to the eye than the lower orbital bone (where wrinkles reside). Most morning puffiness, as mentioned earlier, is the result of hydrostatic pressure, as water collects in pouch "reservoirs" when you're in the prone position. Add another pillow if you must, but don't dispense with the night cream!

Speaking of pillows, some women have told me they actually refrain from putting anything at all on their faces at night, for fear of staining the pillowcase. I always tell them, stains can be washed away, wrinkles cannot! However, even with today's lighter, more readily absorbed formulations, its always a good idea to blot lightly.

Serious Measures

Yes, there's a lot you can do to restore skin texture and tone beyond normal maintenance and moisturizing. You can have collagen injected into the deepest crevices; you can have fatty pouches melted away; droopy skin can be cut, tucked, sanded, and scraped. These are clinical measures, and we'll go over all of them in Chapter Eight.

But, for now, the most "serious" noninvasive measure to change the look of skin is the topical application of Retin-A. Although originally approved by the FDA as a prescriptive acne medication, dermatologists began using it to diminish skin wrinkling—and it worked!. Before you rush off to the doctor, however, there are a few things you should know about it.

Vitamin A, a fat-soluble compound, is crucial to the skin's health. A vitamin A derivative, retinoic acid (patented as Retin-A) alters skin physiology by actually penetrating deep into the dermis and increasing the rate at which new skin cells form, something, remember, a night cream or any other cream cannot do. In addition, Retin-A is believed to speed up production of collagen and elastin. Retin-A appears to retard and reverse the effects of photo-

damage by diminishing wrinkling, fading brown spots, stimulating capillary growth, and giving the skin a rosier, livelier complexion.

That's the good news. But there have been documented drawbacks. First, for any results to become apparent, it can take several months, or even years, of treatment. During that time, your skin may react in unfavorable ways to the drug. Retin-A can dry and irritate skin, causing it to burn, peel, and redden. And the anti-aging effects last only as long as you continue to take the drug. Your skin reverts to its former condition when you discontinue use.

If you and your dermatologist decide you are a good candidate for Retin-A therapy, it's essential that you are scrupulous about using a moisturizer and a good sunblock with an SPF of 15 or higher every day, because the drug thins the skin and increases cell turnover rate.

Several pharmaceutical companies are currently developing modifications and vitamin A–based "cosmeceuticals" in the race to win FDA approval. Time-release encapsulated Retin-A, compatible moisturizer creams, yeast compounds, and fruit acids are all things to watch for at your local drugstore or cosmetic counter soon. In the meantime, you must speak to your dermatologist.

quick fix

The best time to apply moisturizer is fresh out of a shower or tub, when the bathroom is still steamy. And don't forget the rest of you: Hot water robs skin of moisture, so always, always use body cream after bathing.

Alpha-Hydroxy Acids

The newest stars of the skin-repair circuit are alpha-hydroxy acids, derivatives of natural carbohydrates such as sugarcane, citrus fruits, apples, grapes, and lactic acid. Much gentler than Retin-A, these natural wonders encourage skin cell sloughing, breaking up the intercellular "glue" that causes dead surface cells to clump together. Fresh cells rise to the surface as the skin's bottom layer is "plumped." The result? Texture is improved, fine lines and wrinkles are minimized, and even age spots are lightened, when an alpha-hydroxy is combined with a bleaching agent, such as Hydroquinone. After twenty years, alpha-hydroxys are no longer restricted to prescriptive use only. Now they're finding their way into both expensive skin-care preparations and drugstore cosmeceuticals. Manufacturers are hastening to develop formulations with alpha-hydroxy acids in varying concentrations for different parts of the body. The sun- damaged skin of the lower body, for instance, has a different irritation threshold than the face and neck.

It All Depends on How You Look at It

The old saying "Beauty is in the eye of the beholder" becomes even more valid as we get older. If you don't believe in drugs or drastic measures to restore a more youthful appearance, you have to rely on the art of illusion. And that's basically what the rest of this book is all about. But there's a fine line between illusion and deception. In beauty, illusion is a subtle art, utilizing the play of light and shadow. Deception is heavy-handed, an obvious attempt to hide what the eye sees. Unfortunately, the quickest way to call attention to any problem is to try to cover it up. Even in the case of dark shadows or pigment discolorations, at best you try to blend them in with your predominant skin tones. You never try to "hide" them!

So this book is about beauty by illusion and beauty by technique. Once you know precisely how to redefine the new structures of your face (wrinkles and all) and compensate for the effects of aging, you'll have illusion down to a science!

starting over

take a new look at makeup

c h a p t e r 3

As a professional makeup artist, I am often amazed to find that the women I work with own more makeup than I do! And why? You need only what works for you, nothing more. Yet some women tend to *collect* makeup. After a few years of cosmetic clutter in your life, finding the right colors, the right caretakers, can be a bit confusing. You have to simplify to discover what really works and what doesn't.

When you clean out your shelves, you may find a color or two that you used to love, but can't go near now. The truth is, it probably did look good on you once. But, in addition to oxidation, which affects the product's color, your skin tone may have changed since the last time you wore it (remember, skin can become sallower, duller, with time); your hair may be a different color; your whole makeup palette may have changed. Or it may simply be a different time of the year. When you learn to use color to accommodate changes, rather than mask them, your confusion will end.

Beauty by the Month

The environment is part and parcel of how you look; your skin—your complexion—goes through subtle changes all year through. In the winter, you may become noticeably paler; freezing weather causes small blood vessels near the skin's surface to constrict in order to conserve warmth. When blood flow is diminished, color fades from your face. And that's not all. Skin is most vulnerable, most sensitive during winter months. Both wind and heated air remove moisture from the surface of the skin, changing its texture and affecting the way makeup looks on you. In low humidity, skin begins to harden and lose flexibility—even after only a few hours!

If you've made the move to a warm, moist, tropical paradise—beware! First, of unrelenting sun; second, of the decline in the precipitation levels your skin was used to before the move. Sun accentuates the drying effects of air, and there's a higher percentage of UV rays where it's most direct. Higher altitudes or southern and southwestern locations provide less protection from the atmosphere.

As environment changes, skin changes, it's as simple as that. And sometimes what's going on around you can be downright hostile. Your skin can be so irritated by chemicals in the air, pollution, allergens, ozone, and tobacco smoke that it gradually deteriorates. Free radicals, those hyperactive molecules formed by just such environmental hazards, set about their business of destroying certain cells, including skin cells. The point is, where you live and what you expose yourself to will inevitably have a significant effect on the condition of your skin.

Climate-Controlled Beauty

By choosing your cosmetics with care it is possible to devise a strategy for combatting changes in the air *before* they become changes on your face! While it's silly to collect too much makeup, it does make sense to have seasonal alternatives in your cosmetic wardrobe, especially when there's such a variety of formulations to choose from. Each type has its own reason for being, its own specialized ingredients to keep skin in balance. If you let different formulations work for you, *when and where* they should, you'll get a real beauty bonus.

First, let's go through the basic makeup products, that handful of essential beautifiers that most women wouldn't leave home without. The Big Four are: Base, Blush, Eye Makeup, and Lipstick. I'll tell you what to look for in terms of texture and benefits as the seasons and your skin—change.

> # quick fix
> When your face becomes more tan than your neck (or vice versa!), blend the two color zones with a bronzer, then apply your regular base on top.

The Beauty of Base
It Does More Than You Think

Believe it or not, some women are actually afraid of base. Some claim they don't need it, or they've never used it in their lives, or their skin doesn't react well to it. But the real reason may be that they've never found one they're comfortable with. If that's you, it's time to take a fresh look at base.

The right base makes every woman, young or old, look more beautiful. Have you even seen a "perfect" model without base? I've seen hundreds and there wasn't one whose complexion didn't need to be evened and brightened with base. It's the one makeup product that hides a multitude of imperfections: uneven pigmentation, freckles, splotches, blotches, oily shine, dark circles, minor blemishes, you name it. Base unifies and perfects the complexion. But, more than that, it acts as a protective layer for the skin—especially those bases with sunscreen. It also smooths the surface of the skin so other color goes on more evenly and stays on longer.

A complete makeup wardrobe contains several different types of bases. Comfort is the most important determining factor in your selection of a base, but comfort levels vary with temperature, humidity, activity, and even your health. All of these things modify the reaction of your skin.

quick fix
Use a latex sponge for the most precise application of a base to cover imperfections, redness, or blemishes.

How to Select the Right Base for You

If you have shopped for bases formulated for oily, dry, or normal skin, you probably know that a moisturizing cream base is good for dry skin; water-based, lightweight liquid bases are good for oily skin; and a powder compact or balancing base is good for normal or combination skin. But today there are so many other options! There are sheer "sport" bases, basically a color suspension in water; aerated mousse bases that apply quickly and cover without thickness; "whipped" cream bases, which have a lighter consistency than conventional creams; tinted moisturizers offering more treatment than color; and a host of "specialist" bases for oil and acne control, or reducing irritants.

So what to do? Shop for texture, comfort, appearance, and color. None of these are things that can be determined by rubbing a dab on the back of your hand in a store. First of all, the skin on the back of your hand has little in common with the skin on your face. It's thinner, probably a different color, and definitely drier. Secondly, the lighting at a department store cosmetic counter is too artificial. You have to see what you look like in daylight, you have to feel the product on your face. You have to live with it for a few days.

Beyond skin condition, the time of year is equally influential in formulation selection.

Winter The richness of an oil-based cream formulation protects the skin and shuts the cold out. It's more comforting to skin stinging from chill winds. During the dreary days of winter avoid beiges with a gray undertone; opt instead for a luminous shade lightened by a pinch of pink, one close to your own natural skin tone.

Spring It's time to begin lightening up a bit. Switch consistencies and try a base with a fluid texture (it doesn't have to be in liquid form, as long as it is lightweight and moves easily on the skin). As spring light tends to be more golden than winter's, go as pink/beige as you can in your color palette. Opt for a little sheerness and let your skin show: Apply your base with a moistened sponge.

Summer At this time of year you may think you need nothing at all, but that's where you're wrong. Think of summer base as a lightweight sunshield. Even with SPF protection built in, your skin tone will change in the summer, and so should your base shade. Choose a healthy, caramel-y shade that suggests sun. Color tip: If you insist on acquiring a tan over the summer, reflect it in your base by mixing two tones together—one darker, one lighter—gradually increasing the depth of the shade from April to June, decreasing it from September to October. And look for the lightest, *driest* formulations: solid compact bases that you can stroke on with a dry sponge, or liquids that dry on the skin as the water content evaporates. Oil-based formulations would be wrong now, as they tend to "slide" right off moist skin. Tinted, transparent gel moisturizers or lightweight powder bronzers are good alternatives to base when it's simply too hot or too muggy to coat the skin. Check for SPF protection of at least 4. For total blockage, you may wish to apply your own lightweight moisturizing sunblock before applying your base.

> # quick fix
> If you have to camouflage, play with different formulations of the same shade for the most invisible result.

Fall Nothing looks fresher in the fall than a matte makeup. Summer's radiance is over, and it's time for a more sophisticated approach. But don't forget that the moisture content in the air is lessening, and your skin is beginning to thin as weather cools. It needs a replenishing base, one with moisturizing capability. Try a cream base, or a solid cream powder compact, and apply with a wet sponge for greater coverage.

Texture by Skin Type

You should also consider the quality of your skin when you select a base—or any cosmetic! Very fair, delicate skin needs the invisible coverage of fluid products, capable of blending with the fine grain of the skin. As this type of skin tends to be drier as well, it responds best to lighter-textured formulations that are richly moisturized. Thicker, oilier skin often needs heavier coverage that masks tiny flaws and imperfections. Yet it often doesn't need the lubricating benefits of oil-based creams. If your skin is of this type, you must find a base between a light liquid or sheer mousse and a too-rich cream. Compact powder cream bases or oil-free matte liquids will provide good coverage for you.

Eyes Right
Or Everything Could Go Wrong

No matter how skillfully a woman applies makeup to the reast of her face, the wrong eye makeup can ruin a look faster than anything. Expressive eyes are the focal point for the whole face. Unfortunately, they're the first place to show signs of aging. If eye makeup is overdone, it can make you look hard, tired, older—or all three. So why take the chance? Why wear any makeup at all on the eyes? Because there are some very good reasons for doing so. Properly applied, eye makeup draws attention away from skin deficiencies,as it helps define brows and lashes that lighten with age.

Eye enhancement is as much a part of finishing your look as anything else, because it brings all other makeup into balance. You wouldn't wear base and blusher without lipstick. Leaving the eyes "naked" when you're wearing other makeup creates the same unbalanced effect.

How to Select the Right Eye Makeup for You: Cream Shadow sounds like a good idea for delicate eyelid skin. But be careful. Even if cream-based formulations are right for you as a base or blush, creamy, oil-based formulations are *not* for wrinkled skin or drooping lids. The problem is, body heat turns eye makeup oily. Creams collect in the folds—and melt! Cream formulations do have their advantages, however. They're easier to apply, easier to create subtle shading effects with than other eye shadows. If your skin is normal-to-dry, and the lid area is holding up rather well, you might want to give them a try.

Use your fourth, or "ring" finger to apply cream shadow. Put it first in the palm of your other hand to warm it up, then use the soft ball of your finger to pat it gently into place, and sweep across lid. Varying the pressure of your sweep will vary the intensity of the color. Never apply cream shadows over moisturizer or foundation; it will make lids even oilier. "Prime" your lids first with a product formulated specifically for this purpose: Eyelid "fixes" provide a smooth, stable surface for shadow.

Powder Shadows place less stress on the lid, and they're probably the best solution for most women. For this reason, you'll find the most shades in this formulation. One word about color selection: First, keep it as natural as possible—taupes and grays for shadows; light peach, pink, or buff for highlighting; a soft violet inside the crease. Dramatic color is al-

37

ways too much of a contrast on *any* skin by day. If you want to create a vibrant evening face, that's one thing, but for day stick to more subtle, muted tones.Also, avoid any color with iridescence in it. Light-reflecting particles only attract more attention to wrinkled skin, and they never create a smooth, natural appearance.

Powder shadows usually come with their own applicator wands, and these are designed to pick up the color best. Sponge-tip wands work better with some shadows, fuzzy-felt tips work for others, brushes for still others. If you switch to a cotton swab, be aware that you may be leaving 30 percent of the product on the swab! The advantage to cotton swabs, of course, is they are disposable after every use; you don't have to clean them. (The others you do—and should, religiously!) If you do use a cotton swab, rub it very deeply into the powder, collecting as much color as you can. That way, it will stroke on easier; you won't have to press hard to get the color to come off on your skin.

The biggest complaint I hear against powder shadow, in fact, is that it *does* come off. But avoiding "rub-off" is easy. Simply press loose face powder lightly onto the lid before you apply your eye shadow. This absorbs any existing oil (from foundation or skin) that causes color shadow to "slide"off the lid area. Plus, it gives your powder

shadow a texture to grab on to and helps it remain right where you applied it.

I also like to press—lightly—a powder puff to the lid area after finishing. It tends to blend away obvious color demarcation lines, and again serves to set the shadow. Finish by dusting with a clean, bushy makeup brush to remove excess powder. It sounds like a lot of trouble, but the whole procedure takes just a few seconds, and you'll be surprised at the difference it makes. Your eyes will look more naturally shaded, less "made-up."

Liquid Shadow is only lightly moisturizing to delicate lid skin, but it takes moisture with it as it dries. It is also a bit less subtle than powder shadow, because it doesn't blend or "smudge" to create a softer effect. The advantage to this is that it has more staying power. You might wish to stroke a liquid shadow in a pale neutral shade across your entire lid area first, as a "base" for powdered color.

Pencils must be of superior quality to be used near your eyes. Use the best brand you can find and always try it on your skin first in the store (this time, the back of your hand is fine for trying—you're checking for a creamy, smooth glide, not making a color match). If the color doesn't come off the pencil easily, forget it. The beauty of pencils is their

quick fix

Stroke your eye shadow brush across an ice cube before dipping it into powder shadow. Cold shadow glides on better.

blendability. You can increase this by holding the point of the pencil in your hand, or near a light bulb. It's then much easier to stroke on and blend. One caveat: Applying color inside the rim of your eye is not a good idea, particularly if you wear contacts. Color can flake off into the eye. It's also risky to do if you wear glasses—you might miss and go too close to the eye! It may be a good technique for professional makeup artists and young models, but if you're neither, don't try it.

Shadow Crayons, like all color "crayons," are very easy to apply. With a wider tip than a pencil, they release soft, creamy color, in either frost or matte formulations, that glides on easily, with considerable "slip." While they're not for precision-lining, they diffuse and soften color beautifully—and quickly. Just a stroke puts enough color where you want it. Blend it with your fingertip, and you're done!

Whether you choose to apply color to your eyes with shadows or pencils or not, at least one coat of mascara is always a must. It adds definition to the entire area, and serves to give your lashes an eye-opening "lift." Again, there are different formulations to choose from. Find the one you're most comfortable with.

> # quick fix
> Always use a hand mirror, held low, to apply eye makeup. Tilt your head slightly backward and look down into the mirror. It's the only way to see the full lid.

Cake Mascara, once considered "old-fashioned," is now big news again, and for good reason. It's gentler and less drying than waterproof formulations, which may contain alcohol. You can also control the thickness of it, depending on how much, or how little, water you add. (Let the water be from the tap, please, not saliva!) The waxy base of cake mascara is more concentrated, so it coats and conditions lashes better. Another bonus: You apply it with a brush, so you separate lashes at the same time. Nothing is more "age-making" than clumped, dirty-looking lashes. Even if you do prefer to use mascara with wand applicators, always follow up with a little brush, combing between coats.

Waterproof Mascaras are oil-based moisturizers, with film-producing chemicals such as resins or shellacs added to give them greater staying power. If you don't need long-lasting mascara, you don't need these additives on your lashes. However, if water-based mascaras make your eyes sting, you may be able to tolerate these oil-based products.

Treatment Mascaras are a newer idea, and they contain conditioning and strengthening ingredients, a complex of vitamins and amino acids (such as Panthenol and Keratin), in a water-based moisturizing formula. Intended to cling to the hair shaft with color and body that builds up with each coat, they act a little like the softening conditioners you use after shampooing. These formulas are, in general, creamier than traditional mascaras, and are dual-function, providing both color and treatment with a single application.

Gel Mascaras are sheer-color, sometimes no-color, lash coaters that give a very natural, sporty effect. Their main intent is to separate and stiffen lashes ever-so-slightly. If they supply color, it's usually just a soft tint.

Keep in mind that you must throw *any* mascara out once it begins to dry and clump; it's no longer fresh enough to put near your eyes. Exposure to air causes bacteria contamination to form, and that happens every time you slide an applicator out of its sheath. Buy a fresh mascara every two to three months, whether you think you need it or not.

Brush Up on Your Blush

There Are More Ways to Glow

Rosy, glowing cheeks are a signature of good health. This has been so for centuries; you have only to look at the rounded, velvety cheeks rendered by such artists as Botticelli and Rembrandt to know just how long a becoming blush has been considered an integral part of a woman's beauty. Just the right color, carefully applied, illuminates the face and

gives a younger impression. But, even today, there's an "art" to blushing!

Product formulation is just as important a consideration with blush as it is with your base, and again, the texture of blush you use may change with the seasons to give you greater transparency in summer, creamy encouragement in winter. When you select a blush to complement the rest of your makeup, a good rule to remember is *wet on wet, dry on dry.* A cream blush, for instance, blends better with a moisturizing foundation. A powder blush has more punch when applied *over* a dry powder.

Waxy products in stick form provide a protective coating for the skin; creamy products add additional moisturizing. Sheer, see-through gel-based products don't slide into wrinkles, yet they often deliver potent color. Compact blush powders are convenient and portable, ideal to carry for touch-ups. With so many different formulations to choose from, think first of giving your skin what it needs.

How to Select the Right Blush for You:
A Cream Blush is the best friend to dry or damaged skin. It's oil-based, so it provides a degree of lubrication, and it slides easily over the skin, never collecting in wrinkles. It also slides easily off the skin, so you must "set" it with a light press-in of powder, brushing away all excess.

Often, cream blushes tend to "harden" in their containers. Renew the surface by scratching with a cotton swab, and hold it in the palm of your hand (or near a light bulb) before applying in order to warm and soften it.

Apply cream blush first to the palm of your hand, then to your face. Never dab it on your skin directly, or you'll have clown cheeks.

A Gel Blush is the sheerest form of blush coverage, but it tends to stain the skin on contact, and if you spot it directly onto your cheeks, you'll get a wonderful polka-dot effect that won't blend away. To avoid this, always apply a gel blusher over moisturizer. This provides double benefits, both making the gel more blendable and combatting its drying effects. Gels are more suitable for normal-to-oily skin than they are for drying skin.

Powder Blushes are the most popular, most prevalent of all. You'll find more colors, more formula variations, more compact configurations with this type of product than with any other. But that doesn't necessarily make it right for you. Most good cosmetics lines will offer the shade you want in alternative formulations. You do want a powder blush in your makeup wardrobe if your skin is moist enough to accept it, and not deeply wrinkled. It's simply more convenient for on-the-go touch-ups. And a powder blush also adds a nice sophistication to evening makeup. But if you don't have a drop of other

quick fix

Don't let blush "sit" on top of cheeks; dust lightly with colorless powder and blend.

makeup on, beware. Applying powder blush to a clean, fresh face can give you a bright flash of color. It's best to put powder blush on over powder—dry on dry—or it will "grab." And always dust off powder blush with a second—clean—brush. This helps to blend the color in and keep it from accumulating along the lines of your face.

Bronzer Blushes aren't as new as you might think, but they're getting more attention now as "safe" alternatives to a suntan. The difference between a bronzer and a normal blush is a higher saturation of color in a natural, brown-based shade. Some bronzers, particularly for men, actually contain dyes. The color is definitely bronzed, and it often goes on deeper than it looks in the compact or tube. Bronzers can be sheer or semitransparent in cream, gel, or powder formulations; the idea is not to coat the skin with thick, dark color, but to give the illusion—the natural glow—of a tan. Some bronzers actually simulate the glow with frost particles. These reflect light and make your face sparkle in the sun, which is not exactly what a "natural" tan does, but at a distance you do seem to glow. I prefer matte formulations that have some moisturizing properties, instead. These let the glow come from soft, shining skin.

(Autobronzants, or self-tanning bronzers, are

another story altogether. And they're really not part of the blusher category. These products are also called "pre-sun" tanning bronzers, and they actually contain an accelerating agent such as Tyrosin to stimulate melanin production. Unlike earlier dyes and stains, they don't coat color onto the skin, they help your skin *develop* a tanning color. Many promise you the tan you want in just a few hours without any sun exposure at all. Just be very careful in application to avoid a "patchwork" or streaked effect, especially with repeated use.)

Lip Service
Let Treatment Do the Talking

Without a doubt, your lips are the most sensitive area of your face. The nerves there make them disproportionately responsive to pain. If for no other reason, that's argument enough for wearing lipstick—at all times. The waxlike bases protect lips from drying out and offer fairly good sun immunity. Many now contain sunscreening ingredients to add to their protective effectiveness.

But, of course, there are other reasons for adding color to the mouth. It provides a secondary focal point that balances the eyes; it energizes the face; and it gives us something attractive to look at.

Add a bright spot of color to your face, and everything bad seems to go away!

How to Select the Right Lip Product for You:
Lipstick contains pigments in an oil-wax base. They're shaped into the familiar "bullet" form with enough stabilizers and stiffening agents to prevent meltdown. The pigments in lipstick do provide a barrier against UV rays, and some contain added sunscreens. Those that promise "permanent" color often contain staining dyes that adhere to lips long after the moisturizing elements wipe away.

Frosted Lipstick starts with the same basic formulation, but adds pearlizers to the pigment. Shine may take attention away from tiny lines, but it's not for seriously crinkled lips. Add just a dot of frost (or a clear, transparent gel) to the center of your bottom lip, taking care that it doesn't "bleed" into lip creases. Stay away from any lipstick that "moves."

Lip Gels and Glosses have a different consistency than formed lipsticks, with less wax in the formula. This makes them more transient, less long-lasting. They're best used to enhance color, applied over a "base" of lipstick. Most gels have a little lanolin or derivative added for

quick fix

It's easier to get a good supply of color on a lip brush if you use a small spatula to take the color from the stick, working it into a creamy consistency in the palm of your hand. Then saturate the brush with the softened lip color.

shine, liquidity, and intensity. Some gels glide on from brush or sponge-tip applicators, while others come in compact form and are better applied with a brush than with a sticky finger. One word of caution: A little gloss goes a long way.

Cream Powder Lipsticks blend the smoothness of a moisturizing product with the staying power of a powder, and set lip color in the same way that translucent powder sets foundation. Although they feel a little dry to the touch, they do have a creamy "play." They come in matte or frosted formulations. For precise lip definition, always apply with a brush, taking care to even out color so that it doesn't accumulate in lip lines.

Moisturizing Lipsticks are the ideal solution for instant delivery of moisture to dry, parched lips. Although all lipsticks moisturize to some degree, those clearly identified as moisturizing lipsticks contain ingredients specifically intended to augment the hydration process in both matte and lustrous formulations. Some are water-binding emulsions, some are formulated with soothing vitamins and vegetable oils, some with humectants to further "trap" moisture from the air. All feel more comfortable on the lips than drying matte lipsticks. And nothing looks smoother, younger, softer on "over-thirty" lips than a lush moisturizing lipstick.

Lip Pencils are simply eye pencils with a different color palette. The point is—again—to look for the creamiest, smoothest texture. No matter what other type of lip coloring formulation you prefer, always add a pencil or two to your cosmetic lineup, especially if your lip line is beginning to ridge. Lip pencils help to define, line, and "hold" color. Tiny vertical lines around the mouth can best be played down with an even rim of pencil-sharp color. Use a drier formulation of lip pencil here to discourage color from "bleeding" into the ridges. Simply powder over the pencil lightly, blot, and fill in with your normal lipstick selection, just to the inside rim of the penciled line.

Lip "Fix" products treat your lips to special care, conditioning them and softening them before you apply any color at all. Some actually smooth and plump fine lines, filling in tiny crevices. As a plus, they'll keep your lipstick "in line," holding on to it to prevent bleeding and feathering. How do they work? They're formulated with a film-producing ingredient that actually prevents creamy color from falling between the cracks!

In each makeup classification, the formulations you finally settle on are always a matter of personal choice. But with so many varieties to choose from, don't lock yourself into those you've always used. Keep experimenting. You may find some that better complement your changing skin texture, your changing coloring, your changing beauty.

base checklist

Your base wardrobe should include:

☐ **Base a tone lighter than the color of your skin**

☐ **Loose, transparent colorless powder without shine or emollients to "fix" base with a matte finish**

☐ **A moisturizing concealer stick**

☐ **Pre-moistened latex sponges to meld the pigments of the base with those of your skin**

☐ **A big powder puff or a synthetic recycled sponge (dry) to use as a powder puff**

☐ **A full, bushy brush to "dust off" excess powder, keep makeup looking fresh all day**

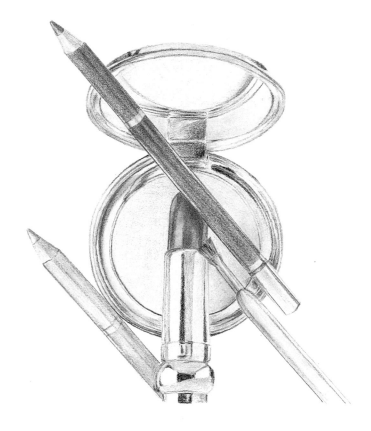

lip checklist

Your lip makeup wardrobe should include:

☐ **A creamy, moisturizing lip color**

☐ **Two lip pencils: a corrective light brown and a red or bronze in a shade close to your lipstick**

☐ **A flat lip brush for impeccable finish**

eye checklist

Your eye makeup wardrobe should include:

☐ **Three colors in a compatible palette: for instance, brown, salmon, beige—or any harmony close to the color of your skin**

☐ **A creamy mascara in brown or charcoal gray**

☐ **A brown or black eye pencil, and a gray, auburn, or blond shading pencil**

☐ **A pink/beige concealer**

☐ **A lash separator brush/comb**

☐ **Cosmetic cotton swabs**

☐ **A fine eyeliner brush**

☐ **A flat, short-bristled blending brush**

☐ **A big, bushy powder brush**

blusher checklist

Your blusher wardrobe should include:

☐ **Three formulations: cream for dry skin, gel for a transparent finish, and powder for evening makeup**

☐ **Two colors: a brown/beige for shadowing and a pink or fresh coral for coloring**

☐ **A blush brush with a rounded top and white bristles (so you can see the actual amount of color you are applying to your face!)**

☐ **A long-handled blender brush, with wide, fan-like bristles, again in white**

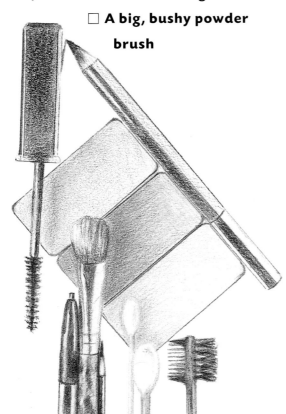

the basic makeup

putting products into practice

Now that you can recognize the characteristics of basic cosmetic formulations, it's time to experiment. If you've never used so many cosmetic products to do your makeup before, don't worry. You'll see just how beautiful you can be, and still look as natural as you like. You're not going to "paint an inch thick," as Shakespeare's Hamlet put it. That's never the sign of a good makeup. But because mistakes are more pronounced on mature skin, you should learn to think of applying your makeup as a gentle "art." And that means assembling the right materials, and taking the time to apply them properly.

There is no mystery to application; simply observe a few general anti-aging rules. The first one is: Less is always more. Thick, dark, unblended lines look much too harsh. Heavy coats of mascara make your eyes look tired. Brilliant blush only makes the rest of your face pale by comparison. Sparkly frosts accentuate every line and wrinkle.

The best makeup is a soft, natural, unobtrusive makeup that doesn't compete with your face or features.

The second rule is: Go against the grain! Never place any color or highlight in direct parallel with a wrinkle or a line; you must break the downward lines with roundness and upward angles.

In the next chapter, I will show you very specific placement techniques for adjusting any architectural imbalances in the structure of your face. But first, here are the ground rules for daily beauty—an effective, step-by-step routine that will allow you to create a perfect, natural-looking makeup. If you choose to customize your makeup to correct or emphasize individual features, it's only a matter of modifying these essential techniques.

daily makeup technique

1 m o i s t u r i z e

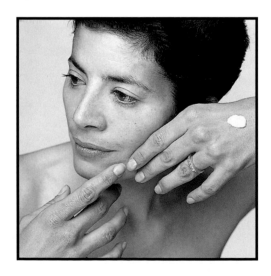

This is the essential first step of preparing your skin to accept color smoothly. Put the moisturizer on the *back*, not in the palm, of your left hand (or your right hand, if you are left-handed). This frees up *both* hands so you can turn your moisturizing moments into a mini massage. Sweep upward (from the base of your neck, please; it's part of your face!) with light, stimulating strokes, one hand following the other. Press lightly in soft circular motions from the bridge of your nose, outward along the orbital bone, continuing around and above your brow bone. If you do this every morning your skin will feel softened, soothed, *and* refreshed—triple beauty benefits in one easy step!

2 b l o t

This is crucial to the "staying power" of your makeup. Every bit of excess moisturizer should be cleared off the skin. But don't drag a tissue across your face, wiping at it like you would a piece of furniture. Simply open a tissue flat, place it over your entire face, and press—lightly—with your fingertips all over until you see excess oil absorbed. Every time you blot, this is the procedure to use.

3 a p p l y   b a s e

Warm a small amount of liquid or cream base in the palm of your less dominant hand. In a few seconds it will reach skin temperature, which makes it easier to smooth onto the skin. For a sheerer day-time texture use a damp sponge to apply base; work the sponge into the base, then fold it and tap it lightly against the face. You don't want to "squeeze" the sponge on the skin, or you'll get a little puddle of color! Start at the center of your face and move to-ward the hairline so the heaviest con-centration of product goes where you need it and less ends up in your hair. Don't forget to blend the base from jawline to neck. After you've finished applying the base, blot again.

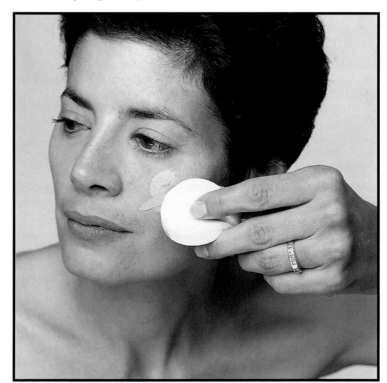

4 hide and highlight

Makeup is simply the law of dark and light. Any area of your face that recedes (furrows, creases, hollows) should be brought out with light. But *only* the indentations, please. If you apply a lightening concealer too recklessly, it will only emphasize pouches and bags by bringing them forward.

Warm your concealer by applying it to the palm of the hand first, then use a fine brush to place a little lightening at the forehead, each corner of the eye, in under-eye hollows, and just beneath the center of the eyebrow. If you have noticeable lines from nose to mouth, start at the corner of your nose and lightly brush concealer within the crevices. Add a dot at the center of your chin, and lighten up mouth corners as well. As they begin to fold down, they cast a very unhappy shadow!

Blend and meld the texture of the concealer with the rest of your makeup by dipping your little finger into a bit of base and pressing lightly—*delicately*—over all concealer lines.

5 powder down

Unify everything with the softening effect of powder. Use a puff or a big pad of cotton, torn from a roll. Dip it in the powder, then press on the face with a gentle, rolling motion. Lastly, use your big, fluffy brush and dust *everywhere,* to remove all powdery excess.

6 add a dash of lash

It's not too soon to apply mascara; two to three light coats are better than one quick, thick application at the end. This also allows time for each coat to dry thoroughly, reducing sticky, clumpy build-up. When you begin, apply only to the tips of the lashes to make them appear thicker. Later coats can get to the roots. Always, after each coat, separate lashes with a spiral separator or eyelash comb. Start just at the lashline, and roll down over the lashes.

makeup don'ts

- Stay away from too-deep eye shadow colors and dark brows.
- Shun brown, earthy-colored blush.
- Never extend your blush into your hairline.
- Never apply lipstick without a lip brush!

51

7 make eyes

The trick to soft, natural shadowing is *subtle layering.* It's a series of strokes, one building on top of the other, from lash line to brow line, with color gradually becoming less intense as you approach the brow. Begin by powdering the entire lid area with a big, bushy brush to give color something to cling to, or smooth on eye shadow primer. Now using your applicator or a cotton swab, stroke on a neutral contouring shadow (gray, taupe, or soft violet) with your applicator or a cotton swab starting just above the lashes at the *outer* corner of the eye. Sweep it one-quarter to one-half of the way across your lid, decreasing the pressure as you go so the color becomes lighter as it nears the center. Without putting more color on the applicator, make a second stroke slightly above the first, then above that, then above that. When you have almost no color left on your applicator, go all the way up to the eyebrow. If you've made the color too intense at any point, flip to the clean side of the applicator and remove some.

Next, use a lighter, neutral color (ivory, buff, yellow, beige) and reverse the procedure. Begin at the inner corner of the eye and sweep outward, overlapping the deeper shade slightly. Then sweep it up to the center of the brow bone. A healthy highlight of pink or peach may be added just under the brow bone, all the way across.

Finally, the three "territories" should be unified, edges blended, with a soft dusting of powder. Use a smaller, square-edged eye shadow brush to confine loose, transparent powder to the area, and apply sparingly! Simply dip the brush in the powder, tap it against the back of your hand a few times to shake off excess, then sweep it on—and off—the lids, collecting excess powder as you go.

8 define with eyeliner

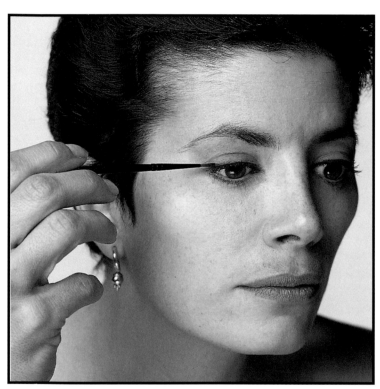

Eyeliner is often forsaken by women who want a "natural" look, but applied correctly, it can give you all that—and more. A darker tone just at the base of the lashes adds wonderful definition, makes lashes look longer, and actually helps correct eye shape, if needed.

It doesn't have to be a harsh line. It doesn't even have to be a fine line (*very* hard to draw, if you have any problems with your hands). In fact, it doesn't even have to be eyeliner at all!

For a softer, smudge-able effect, I prefer to use eye shadow. Simply moisten a corner of it, use a small brush, and stroke a quick, semi-thick line three-quarters of the way from the outside corner of your lashes. Now place a cotton swab at the top of the line and "roll down," drawing the color toward the lashes until it's as thin as you like.

I don't suggest using powder under the lower lashes; there's too great a risk of it smudging. Instead, use a soft eyeliner pencil. Stroke the color first into the palm of your hand, then apply with a brush. If it's creamy enough, the brush will pick the color up easily; if it isn't—you shouldn't be using it!

Color tip: Your eyeliner should harmonize with your shadow palette, but it doesn't have to match exactly. For day, use a neutral such as light gray or brown. For night, you might want to add eye-dazzling color—a teal, a plum, an emerald green. But do avoid iridescence and black. Black is *not* a "natural" shade; it is what we are trying to *avoid* around the eyes, at all costs!

⑨ bring out your brows

More than any other feature, your brows add expression to your face. Make them dark and heavy, and they change your whole aspect. Make them too light, and your eyes lose importance immediately.

In general, lighter brows are younger-looking (have you ever seen a baby with dark, heavy brows?). If yours are naturally dark, consider having them professionally lightened just a notch or two and see what a face-brightening difference it makes.

Every brow, no matter how perfectly shaped it seems to be, has "bald spots." Browse for yours by brushing all brow hair straight down. Where the line seems to break is exactly where you must fill in with pencil, directly on the skin, not on the brow hair. When you brush the brow up again, it will look naturally filled in. And always use two different color pencils—a brown and a gray for brunettes, a blond and an auburn for blondes. Hair is never a single, solid shade; it has highlights. You can re-create this effect by alternating short strokes in two different shades. It's much more natural.

just say no

■ Never be too busy to be beautiful.
■ Avoid a chalky, cakey look.
■ Shy away from anything that looks artificial.

10 add a natural blush

Obvious cheek contouring is a thing of the past, but working with two colors can lend a nice "lifted" shape to your cheek . . . if done very discreetly. Choose two colors that are fairly close—one deeper, one brighter. Sweep the deeper blush just under the curve of your cheek, extending it up *almost* to the hairline. Apply the brighter shade on the roundness of the cheek, blending it *carefully* with the under color. Powder over everything with a big, fluffy brush to blend the two shades and remove excess color.

As the lines of your face begin to pull down, keep the placement of your blush somewhat high. In some cases, you'll stroke it right up to your temple. But be careful it doesn't slip into your under-eye area. The skin there isn't tight enough to have attention called to it!

Gel and cream blushes should be tapped on lightly with the finger and blended immediately. Powder blushes should be applied with a full, long-handled brush for easier control. Don't use the tiny brushes that come in compacts, except for touch-up emergencies—they

don't allow your hand enough distance from your face for you to see where you're putting the color and their shorter, stiffer bristles never sweep color on as softly. To avoid the mystery of how much color you're applying use brushes with white bristles; if your brush suddenly looks too pink, your cheeks will, too.

🔢 finish with lips

You need to pay particular attention to the mouth now, even if you just quickly dashed lipstick on all your life, because the lips are another dead giveaway of age. They wrinkle, pucker, tend to change shape, and droop at the edges. Time for a little corrective artwork.

First, ignore the creases at the corners. Close your mouth when you are shaping the lips with pencil, and the pencil won't fall into the folds. Redesign the contour of your lips with a light-brownish pencil, correcting all imbalances. Round the shape slightly at the sides, avoiding a harsh V in the center. Lips tend to get thinner as we get older, and strong angles can to look a little witchy. Add a second line just underneath the brown line, using a pencil in a shade close to your lipstick color, and unify the two by patting gently with your finger. Now your mouth is both corrected and outlined. Never try to outline a new shape with a single color. All irregularities will jump out immediately! Use a two-tone process, or don't do it at all.

Use lip pencil to create a perfect outline, correcting the shape if necessary. Fill in your lips with a bright, happy color, using a brush for precise application and start at the center, not at the corners. This way the color will be distributed more evenly and smoothly by the time you reach the edge. And always stay within the pencil line. That's what's going to keep the color from "bleeding" up into tiny lip crevices. Remember, a mouth with a perfect shape and a pretty color is one of the nicest things to look at on a face. Make yours count for all it's worth!

12 powder again

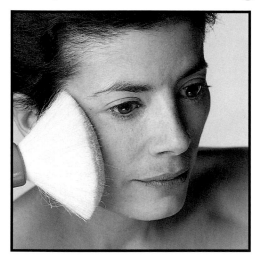

Finally, one last dusting of loose powder, lightly swept over the entire face with a big, full brush, unifies everything, giving you a natural, velvety finish. Don't be heavy-handed; use the brush as delicately as you would your fingertips.

Et voilà! As many steps as this seems, they'll soon become second nature. And anything less would be shortchanging your beauty!

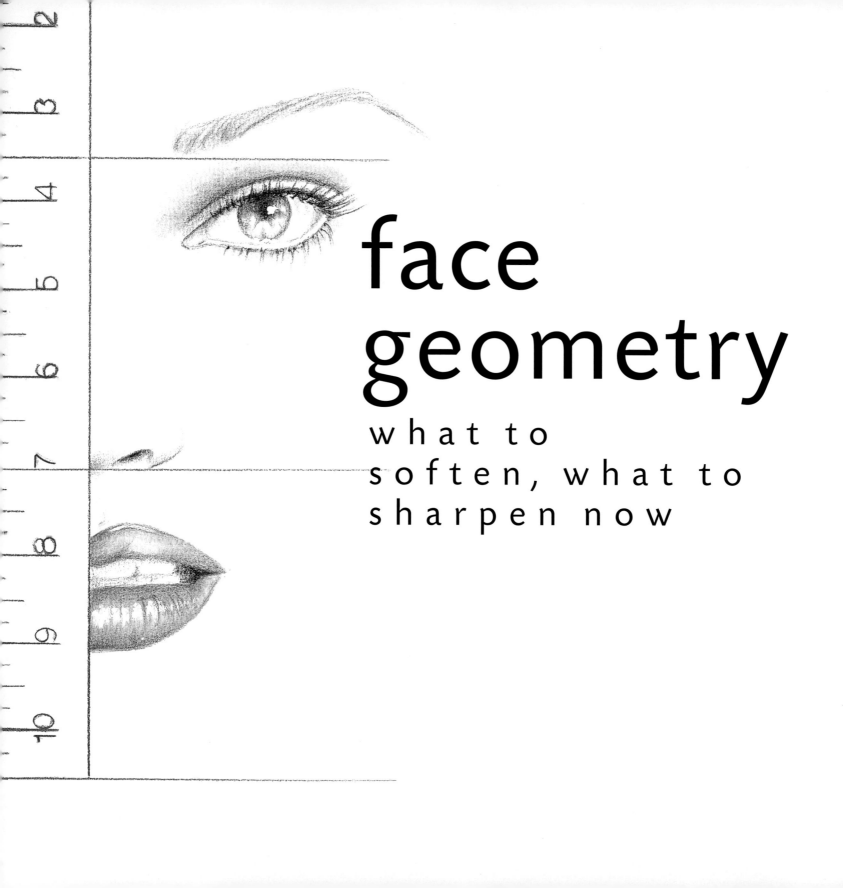

face geometry

what to soften, what to sharpen now

chapter 5

In the previous chapter, we learned the basics of makeup application. And for now that may be the only makeup you need. But as discussed in Chapter One, the topography of your face is changing, and will continue to change, bit by bit, as you get older. You may find that you want to restructure the look of your nose, your chin, your cheek line. Before you think about rearranging things surgically, discover the difference a simple change in makeup placement can make.

Whether you're used to wearing a lot of makeup or a little, you must continue to reassess the way you approach your face. You can get away with unstrategic color placement when your skin is young and firm; you don't have to be precise. However, as you begin to develop your own natural shadows and valleys, you only want to "accentuate the positive." An indiscriminate use of color can be quite unflattering. Daylight is unforgiving, never disguising for a second any flaws in your skin. Night light can be cruelly artificial, robbing your skin of warmth, turning wrong color choices into an aging mask. Color, and correct placement, is what is going to get you through. Like it or not, corrective techniques become more important with every passing year. Casual makeup placement won't bring you the best results you can achieve.

The Law of Dark and Light

Perhaps the most basic principle behind face geometry is this: Shadow diminishes, light augments. If your eyelids are too heavy, a darker shadow will make them appear less droopy, a lighter one will only emphasize the heaviness.

It is wonderful to imagine that we can just put a shadow on something we don't like and it will disappear. But it's not that easy. You must be very careful with shading, or your makeup will have a patchy, splotchy look. Always connect a deeper tone to the surrounding color by blending, blending, blending. A shadow placed beneath the chin or under the cheekbone must artfully disappear into the color of the blush.

And what about light? It works beautiful magic as well. Light can fill wrinkles and ridges (but only if placed inside; otherwise it will make them appear even puffier!). Light can soften undesirable shadows under the eyes, at the corners of the eyes and mouth, and above the lips, where the nose may cast a shadow. Light can also enlarge, making a

the art of

Spot lights: highlighter helps soften deep lines, dark areas.

forehead seem wider, a chin more prominent.

When you add a highlight to your makeup, you must be just as subtle as you are with shadow. Remember, a light always has a central point and a halo. As you lighten a halo toward its edges, it blends with the surrounding color naturally.

Just as you can turn a flat circle into a ball, and a flat square into a cube with proper shading, so you can create new dimensions for your face, eyes,

shading

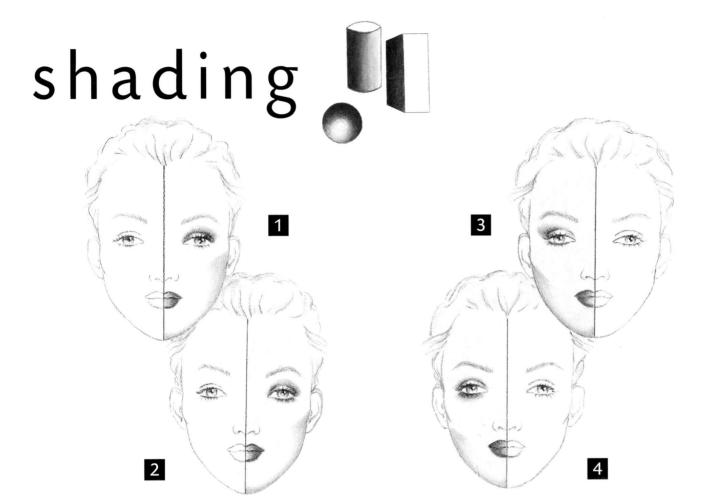

cheeks, lips, and nose by applying the law of dark and light. Case in point: Eye color only on the upper lid (1) elongates a short face. Eye color on both upper and lower lid (2) is in perfect proportion for an oval face. Heavier accenting on the lower lid (3) reduces the appearance of length in a longer face. And putting the color accent on the outer portion of the eye (4) softens a square face.

Adding little spots of "light" to a face is like an instant "lift." It helps to fill wrinkles and ridges, and brightens your whole aspect. No matter what your face shape, there are always certain points where you can add a little light: under the eye; in the center of the forehead; beneath the brow bone; in the corners of the eyes; at the sides of the nostrils; under the lower corners of the mouth; and in the center of the chin. But don't forget to blend!

drag at the mouth and cheek lines, no matter what your face shape.

You can create interior or exterior emphasis with eye shadow as well. The three pairs of eyes at right are actually identical, but by emphasising a different portion of the lid with color and redesigning the brows (see techniques for brow shaping on page 64), it is possible to make them appear more close-set or wide-set.

1

Interior emphasis: redirects attention to features.

The design of the brows, the contour of the mouth and eyes, all create the graphics of your face. And these natural accents can be concentrated on either the interior or the exterior of the face. The popular focus today is on the exterior, yet color emphasis toward the center of the face does serve to alleviate a "flat" appearance and help correct a too-round face (1). A narrow face, in contrast, must place the focus toward the exterior (2). This is also the proper placement for color if you have dark circles under the eye, or obvious downward

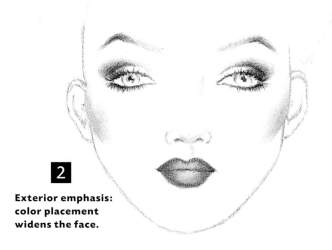

2

Exterior emphasis: color placement widens the face.

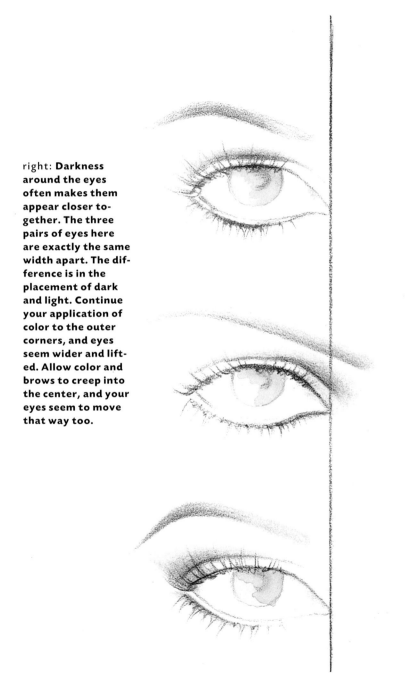

right: **Darkness around the eyes often makes them appear closer together. The three pairs of eyes here are exactly the same width apart. The difference is in the placement of dark and light. Continue your application of color to the outer corners, and eyes seem wider and lifted. Allow color and brows to creep into the center, and your eyes seem to move that way too.**

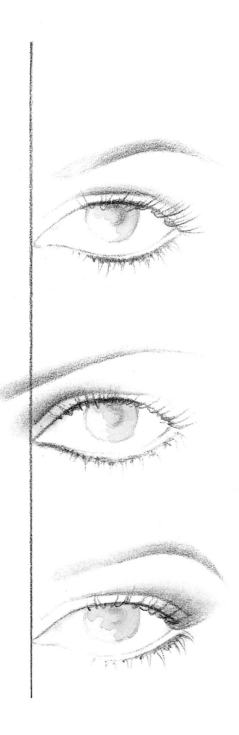

the starting line—

Ask a woman what her most important feature is and she's unlikely to name her eyebrows. Yet this one feature defines every other line of your face. Your brows move. They add expression. If they are not carefully defined, you will lose definition in the entire upper portion of your face.

The line of the brows is the master line of the face; every makeup and contouring placement will be made in relation to these angles, so it is critically important that your brows be shaped correctly. Even if you've never shaped your brows before or considered using a brow pencil, now is the time to start.

Start by recognizing that your brow line is not a straight line at all, but consists of three very distinct elements: an ascending angle, an arch, and a descending angle. By altering the point at which any one of these elements begins, you can alter your entire aspect.

The ideal brow adds lift to the eyes (up is young, down is old), and adjusts the width and length of the face. Making subtle adjustments in the direction of the eyebrow ending or the point at which it leaves the bridge of the nose can open up the center of the face, make a round face seem more oval,

and bring the whole face into sharper focus.

So what is the perfect shape for your brow? Begin by determining the proper placement of the arch. Looking directly into a mirror, hold an orange stick vertically in front of your eye just at the outer edge of your iris. The point at which the stick crosses the brow is where the arch should be (see illustration, left.)

Next, hold the stick vertically at the side of your nostril. This is where a natural brow line should start. Don't tweeze your brows too far behind this line, or you'll end up shortchanging them. (Contrary to popular opinion, overtweezing here will not serve to "widen" the distance between the eyes. It is really the location of the arch that does that.)

Lastly, hold your orange stick diagonally against the base of your nose so that it extends past the outer corner of your eye. Your brow should not go beyond this point (see illustration, opposite.)

Determining the best downward angle, the angle at which the brow descends from the arch toward the temple, is an art in itself. Depending on where you direct the downward slant, your brow actually helps to shape the face (see 1–4, opposite.)

a well-shaped brow

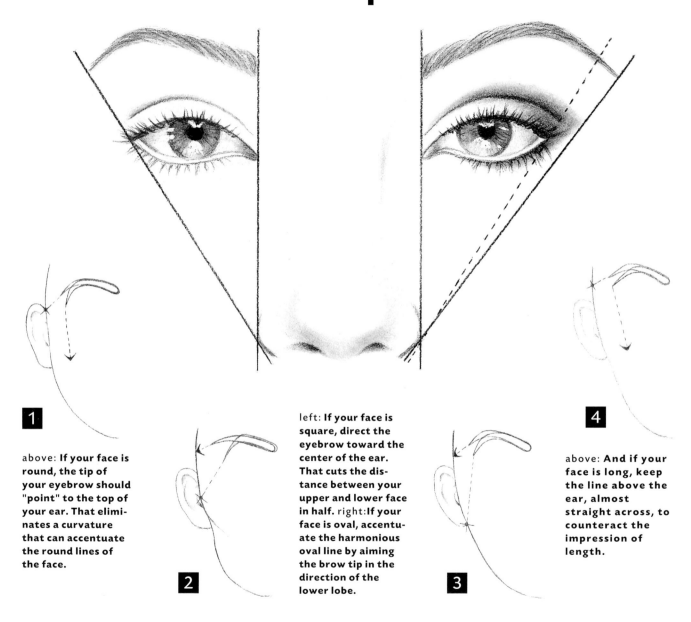

1

above: **If your face is round, the tip of your eyebrow should "point" to the top of your ear. That eliminates a curvature that can accentuate the round lines of the face.**

2

left: **If your face is square, direct the eyebrow toward the center of the ear. That cuts the distance between your upper and lower face in half.** right:**If your face is oval, accentuate the harmonious oval line by aiming the brow tip in the direction of the lower lobe.**

3

4

above: **And if your face is long, keep the line above the ear, almost straight across, to counteract the impression of length.**

charting your course

With a well-defined brow as the anchor, you are ready to discover your natural parallels, the lines that will determine both where contouring should fall as well as the precise location for makeup application.

The principle beind it all is really very simple. Every pleasing pattern in nature is created by harmonious repetitions of parallel lines. Think of the veins on a leaf; a series of waves rippling into the shore; the situations of the landscape. This is the guiding logic behind all makeup alignment. Parallels give an overall harmony to the face, and they should not be ignored.

It is relatively easy to discover your natural parallels. All of them will be based in one way or another on the brow line you've just established. Start by taking a recent full-face photo of yourself, place a piece of tissue or tracing paper over it, and trace the outline of your face from the top of your forehead to the bottom of your chin. This is the blank canvas on which you will be sculpting your new face geometry.

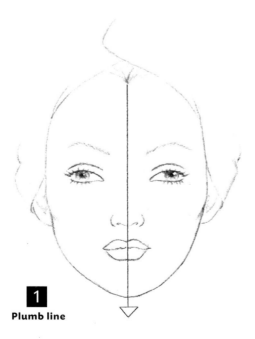

1
Plumb line

■ Begin by drawing a plumb line straight down the center of your face (1).

■ Next, draw your **chin V.** *Any shading you do will be in parallels corresponding to this line.* To find it, align your ruler to the tip of your chin, the arch of your eyebrow, and the hairline; then draw a line connecting all three points (2). As you do this on each side, the resulting V will clearly show you the area that is the center of attention on your face. A wider V angle gives the face more fullness, more openness. A more acute angle narrows it, making you look sadder and older. If your face is closed with a very narrow angle, you can change it easily. Simply reshape your brow moving the arch

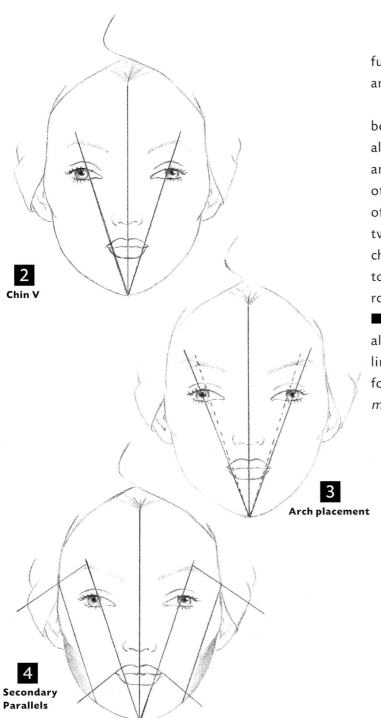

2
Chin V

3
Arch placement

4
**Secondary
Parallels**

further toward the hairline (3) and see how the angle instantly opens up!

To see the precise area in which contouring will be placed, you will need to find the secondary parallel. To do this, extend the line of the descending angle of your eyebrow to the hairline. Draw another line parallel to this one that extends the line of the upper lip to the jaw line. Now connect these two points with a line that is parallel to the first chin V you drew (4). When a darker base is applied to the area falling outside this line, it has a narrowing effect on the face; a shade lighter widens.

■ Lastly, sketch in your **brow V** by aligning a ruler along the ascending lines of the brows. Extend this line from the plumb line to the hairline. Repeat for the other brow (5). *This brow V will determine how and where you apply your makeup.*

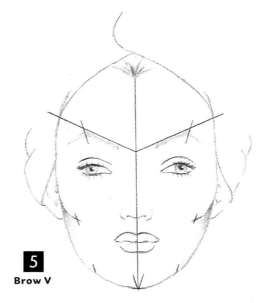

5
Brow V

67

6

Makeup placement

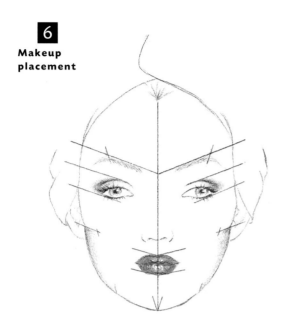

The drawing above (6) shows how these parallels translate into makeup placement. The shadows of the eyes should complement perfectly the brow V line, and the same parallel should define the cheek area and the V of your upper lip. Secondary eye parallels can be drawn from just inside the crease of your lid to the temple, and just under the lower lashes to the temple. Match the angles of these lines to your original brow V, and you'll know exactly where to place eye shadow color—nothing should dip or droop beneath these lines.

This is just a preliminary course in getting the right "angles" for your face. Further parallels will be explored as they apply to each individual face shape. For now, it is enough that you see they can make a striking difference.

What Do These Lines Tell You?

These lines only serve to isolate special areas of your face, areas you may wish to shade or to highlight. If you stay within the lines, the correcting techniques you do will gracefully adapt to your facial structure. To break a line is to create disharmony and contrast. Sometimes that may very well be the desired result. Parallels can be deliberately broken to move attention away from a feature. For instance:

■ With a square jawline, round the curve of your lower lip. To have the lower lip form a parallel line with the jaw only accentuates its squareness (1).

■ With a pointed chin, square off the lower lip, and avoid V necklines to soften the overall effect (2).

■ With a narrow face, avoid accenting the length by squaring the lower lip line (3).

■ When nasal lines and lower lip lines are parallel, offset them by rounding the upper lip (4).

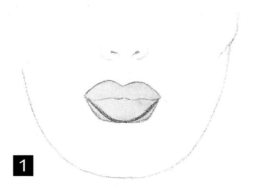

1

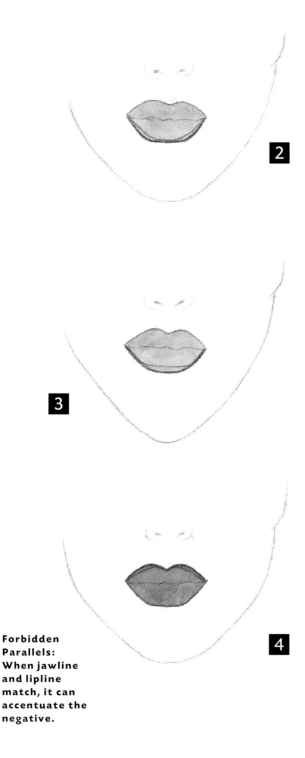

2

3

Forbidden Parallels: When jawline and lipline match, it can accentuate the negative.

4

Putting Theory into Practice

You can guess where color goes, or you can apply it precisely where a professional makeup artist would. Since you are my pupil, I want you to have all the advantages of a private session, and I want you to put color exactly where I would.

The first step in dealing with the new architecture of your face is to find out exactly what the structure is, where the various parallels are, and how the overall shape has changed. Using the same full-face photo of yourself, once again trace the outline of your face from the top of your forehead to the bottom of your chin. Ignore your hair, and see yourself for the first time without its shape-altering effects. It should become quickly apparent if your facial shape is more round, more square, perfectly oval, or long and narrow. These are the four different types we will "plot" corrective strategies for in the upcoming diagrams.

The primary goal of all corrective techniques, of course, is to make the face appear more like a perfect oval. If you are lucky enough to have that "ideal" face shape already, these strategies will simply help to accentuate the positive! Whatever your face shape is, though, the procedure is always based on the two major parallels: First, contour using the chin V as a guideline, then add makeup with the brow V determining placement, and finally add highlights to blend, soften, and focus the entire makeup. Easy as one, two, three!

oval

With an oval face, there is no need for serious re-shaping. Once you know your natural parallels, however, you'll be able to focus attention where you want it, drawing the eye away from aging lines and obvious wrinkles.

Although the basic shape of your face will not change, gravity and lines will shift the focus downward, and this does affect the *perception* of your face shape. To counteract this, accent makeup must

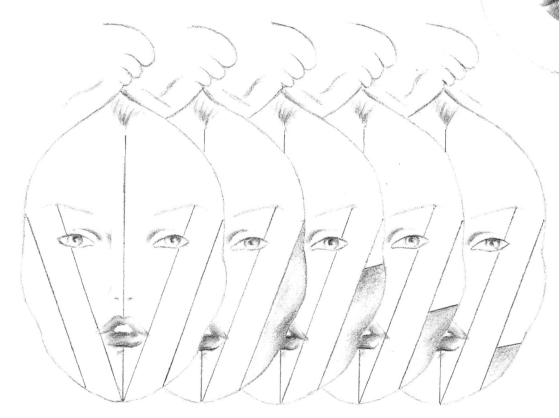

left: **Precise contouring balances facial proportions. Camouflage fullness from jawline to temple, only where necessary.**

be placed just a bit higher. The idea is to bring everything up and away from problem areas.

After drawing your plumb line, open or narrow the angle of your face by changing the placement of the brow arch (1). Use your secondary chin V parallel line as your guide to contour placement (2). To redefine a youthful oval shape, apply contour only to the fullest portion of your face, sculpting a subtle, natural hollow just under the cheekbone (see the five different blush applications, opposite.) Next, draw your brow V line. Drawing the arch of your brows higher (3) will focus attention upwards, away from sag and droop. And, if you follow this important V parallel for eye shadow placement, as you should, everything will automatically be placed higher.

Finally, highlighting can be used to your advantage, not

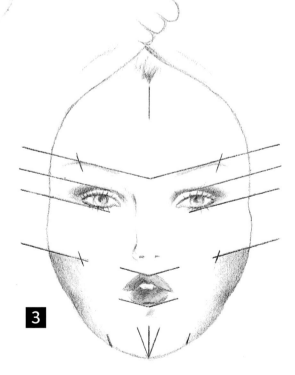

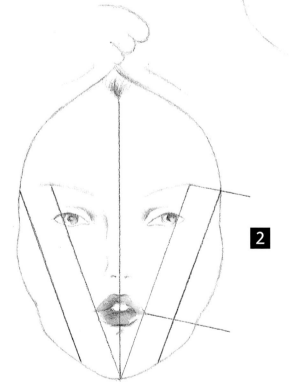

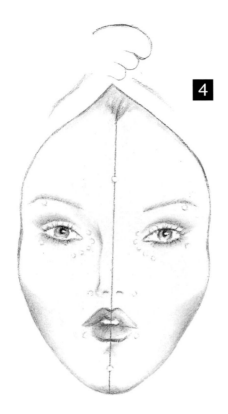

to reshape or resculpt, but to draw attention away from shadows and crevices (4). If you place small dots of a lighter highlight shade at the inside corners of your eyes, for instance, you will offset crow's feet, corner crinkling, and a droopy jawline. If you apply highlights to the outside corners of your eyes, you will bring the focus away from deep naso-labial lines and center-of-the-forehead furrows. It's all a matter of balance.

Other areas to bring a little light to include the middle of the chin, the corners of your mouth, the sides of your nose, the middle of your forehead, the arch of your brow, and the rim of undereye "bags."

square

If the tissue paper tracing of the general outline of your face reveals wide cheekbones and jaw line, you need to concentrate on softening and diminishing the square effect.

It is very important to "open" a square face by increasing the angle of the brow V. To do this, you must move the arch of your brows toward the exterior of your face (1). At the same time, subtly

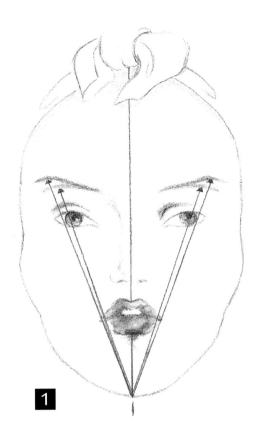

raise the brow line. This will give more importance to the forehead, balancing the dominance of the jawline. As a bonus, higher brows have the effect of diminishing forehead wrinkles. They give the eye something much more interesting to focus on!

Face graphics (the design of shadows and color) should be pushed to the edge. With an "open" face, a concentration of color in the center defeats everything. For exterior emphasis, you need to draw your parallel lines to determine the exact

73

angle of color and contour placement.
Begin with your chin V contour line.
Draw a secondary parallel by continuing from this point down to the jawline (2). This will signal the area to shade, a crucial step in sculpting an overly wide jaw. Apply a shade deeper base from under the jawline to just under the cheekbone. Your blush will stop just at the cheekbone, above the shaded area.

Eye shadowing again echoes the crucial brow V. Follow this parallel and draw an inner lid line, sweeping across the crease and up, and a lower lid line (3). Create a corresponding V at the top of the lips as well. It is very important that all of these lines share the same angle for facial symmetry. Remember nature's perfect parallels? With these lines you have just created a rhythm

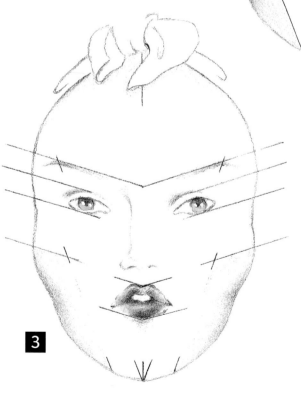

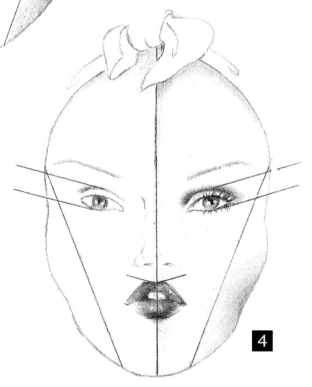

which will be very useful for correct color placement. Now, all you have to do is fill in the blanks!

Apply shadow on the upper lid in the area between the two parallel lines, with emphasis on the outside, rather than the center or interior (4). This will elongate the eye and, by contrast, leave the upper part of the lid looking luminous. Color for the bottom lid should be absolutely parallel to the eye shadow line, gradually thickening as you take it from midway to the outer corner of the eye.

The V of your upper lip will give you an outline for correcting its shape, if you need to add more

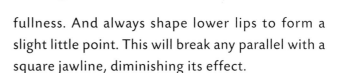

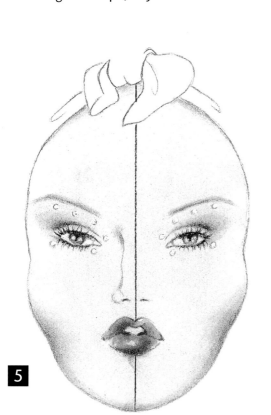

5

fullness. And always shape lower lips to form a slight little point. This will break any parallel with a square jawline, diminishing its effect.

Now you are ready to see the light (5)! Use a lighter, opaque concealer at the center of the forehead, in the nasal fold of the eye, and on the bridge of the nose in order to bring the upper portion of your face into prominence. Use concealer as well to soften severe facial creasing, including the lines from the side of your nose to your mouth. Add a bit of brightness to the center of your chin to offset the width at the sides of your chin. And that's it. Powder, blend, and go!

round

The natural inclination is to correct a round face by simply making it "thin." However, if you raise your forehead, your brows, and your cheekbones through subtle shading, you'll reduce the illusion of roundness much more effectively.

First, it may be necessary to lift and reshape your brows. Brush one of your brows all the way up to see the difference a higher placement makes. Now redraw a brow line above your normal brow,

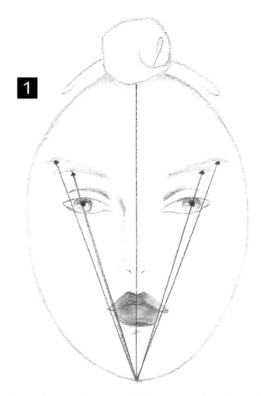

keeping the arch toward the exterior in order to "open" the face (1). Extend the descending line of the brow toward the top of your ear to eliminate accenting the curvature of your face. Keep the distance between your brows as wide as possible. All of these effects will place more focus on the central part of your face, exactly where you want it.

If your new brow shape pleases you, you will have to tweeze away any hairs that don't fall within the new line, and draw the shape in. There's no other way to do it; you can't cover up a brow with makeup base. Don't worry, it will be worth it.

Now that you have redefined the descending

arch of your brow, use this new descending angle to find your contour line. Simply draw a line from temple to chin, parallel to the chin V (2). This is exactly the area you must shade with a deeper tone of base. To reduce roundness even more, you can use a second, subtly deeper color in a small little strip just at the contour of your jawline.

Giving the eyes more attention will also help "lift" the face and place the focus higher. Always place your shadow to the exterior of the eye, following the parallels of your brow V (3). Draw two more lines parallel to the brow V, one from the inner corner of your eye, along the crease and outward, and one underneath your eye. Eyeshadow and a thin undereye line should fall within these parallels. For the face to be in perfect harmony, the V of your lip and the line of your cheek should also be at the same angle as the

2

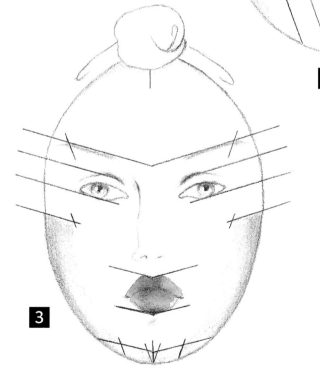

3

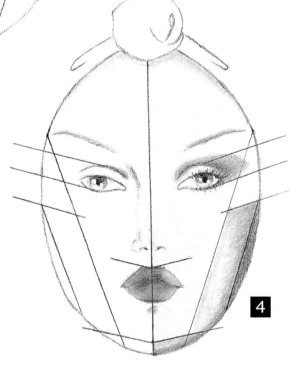

4

eye parallels. Place your blush very high on the cheekbones to elongate the face (4).

If your face is extremely round, it is necessary to lighten the aspect of a heavy chin. To do this, draw two new parallels from the point of your chin to just below the tip of each ear, along the same angle as your chin V. Shade underneath this new V to sculpt the bottom of the face.

Because all lines must focus attention upward on a round face to redistribute its balance, use lights and shadows to create trompe l'oeil tricks (5). For instance, the shadow on your upper lid should be much stronger than the line underneath. Then you

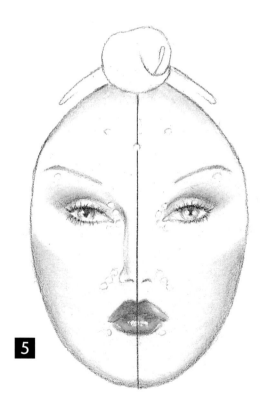

5

will lighten just under the brow bone to give more height to the brow. Bring this light clear down to the eye crease, stopping short of the parallel crease line. A touch of light on the forehead will also put emphasis on the central part of the face. Reinforce the high placement of the cheekbones by lighting just the uppermost angle of where blush will fall.

Don't forget to X-out wrinkles, creases, and under-eye hollows with the artful application of light just in the depressed area. Lastly, unite everything—always—by blending with a powder blush, and no one will be able to spot your face "art."

long

A face that is long and, by nature, narrow tends to exaggerate its shape as the cheekbones hollow with age. Your objective will be to bring the upper and lower portions of your face into harmony.

Begin by looking at your chin V. As it is always necessary to "open" a long face, you should elongate the arch of your brow, moving it toward the exterior, without raising its height (1). The more horizontal your brow is, the better.

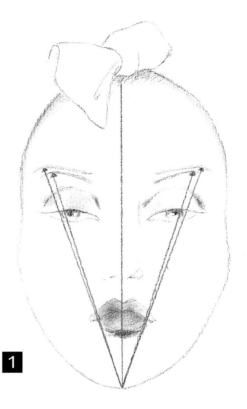

1

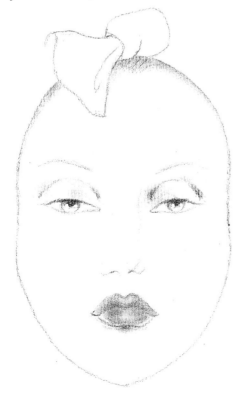

Your contour parallels (the second V line, connecting the descending lines drawn from brow to temple and upper lip to chin) serve to set the limits on shading (2). Ignore the upper area and shade only to underneath the cheekbone to give more importance to the upper part of the face. Shading at the cheek should be placed low (at nose level) to diminish the general appearance of length.

Define your eye shadow parallels by drawing two parallels from your lid crease outward, and along the bottom lid line, both corresponding to the brow V (3). Any color or highlight should be confined within these lines. Keep your graphics away from the center; apply color only from the middle of the eye outward to enlarge the central part of the face.

Use your lip V to create the last set of parallels, important for shading the lower part of the face (4). Follow the ascending angle of your lip V, tracing it out so that it's parallel with your eye lines. Just at the chin point, draw two lines parallel to this, from the cen-

ter plumb line to below the tip of your ears, and you will see what to shade in order to shorten the face. Subtle shading underneath the chin will send attention right where you want it.

Use light to consolidate this effect (5). Highlight the area between brow and eye shadow, and at the outside of the cheekbones. As with shadow color, light can draw attention to the exterior of the

2

3

4

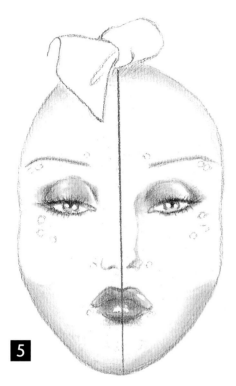

5

face. Use it also to correct any downward lines—the laugh lines between nose and chin, for instance. Everything should be on the "up and up" to correct the length of the face!

the overall effect

Every time you apply your makeup, imagine where your parallel lines will fall. This takes practice, but ultimately it will make your makeup application that much easier. Just remember, your features always determine your makeup style. A strong, dominant face can support a stronger makeup approach. Fine features and translucent skin texture call for delicate, subtle makeup application. If you don't respect the overall character of the face, you will upset your own unity of style. By the same standard, no one feature should stand out. Anything that visually upsets the symmetry and harmony of your face is automatically aging.

combatting the age zones

spot correcting where it counts

chapter 6

The contouring techniques you've just learned create architectural illusions, seeming to change facial contours and structures that may have started changing on *you.* They involve rethinking makeup and color placement, once your face and features have "settled." But because change happens *gradually*, it is sometimes necessary to address individual areas of the face that suddenly seem to be out of balance with your overall youthful appearance. There are definite features and areas that call unwanted attention to themselves, occurring at random and at will.

While your skin follows its own private aging agenda, certain areas do tend to show more pronounced effects of aging than others; I call these the Seven Deadly Age Zones. Give careful attention to each of the following age zones to see if they are unduly influencing your appearance.

zone one the forehead

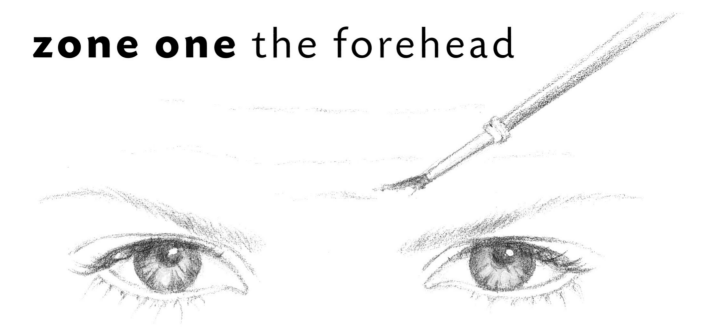

Deeply accented ridges on your brow, either horizontal or vertical, don't necessarily make you look older; you may have had them all your life. But they do have an unpleasant connotation—we don't call them worry lines for nothing! Because their patterns are hereditary, they're usually so deeply ingrained that there's little you can do to make them go away, short of corrective surgery. And yet a few artful techniques will draw the eye away from this area.

First, reconsider your hairstyle. A soft fringe of bangs can do wonders to mask horizontal lines. For deep, vertical "frown" lines, keep the focus higher and off-center by sweeping hair slightly to the side and off the forehead. Of course, avoid bangs altogether if they are totally wrong for your face shape;

you'll only be trading one problem for another!

The forehead is a wonderful place to add light. This will give the upper portion of the face balance and emphasis. But you have to proceed with caution. If you add a dab of highlighter between your brows, you'll only make vertical furrows look deeper. Instead, use a small brush to apply highlighter in the center of the creases, to even out dark and light. I call it filling in the ridges, and you do it *on top* of your base, not underneath. When you powder over, it will all blend in.

You might also try mixing a bit of lavender or light pink eye shadow with a moisturizer cream to create your own high-powered concealer. These tones tend to lighten really deep shadows better than beige or neutral shades.

zone two the brow area

Forehead wrinkles can come right down into the eyebrow, or the brow can develop its own, just at the outer limits of the arch. And a crease here tends to echo upward two or three times! Now that you know how the brows provide an important focus for the entire face, you will want them to be as wrinkle-free as possible. Fortunately, it's easy to cover up the creases here. Simply march the brow right into them. Fill in your brow to the point of the wrinkle on top of the arch. When it becomes part of the brow, it disappears!

Another age-cheater: Sculpted, highly arched brows look wonderful on models now, but wait this trend out. Eyebrow fashions change; the important thing is to find the most flattering look for your own face. Thin brows can be more severe than sophisticated on an older woman, so take it easy with the tweezers! The softer the brow line, the younger it looks. Do your best to add a bit of fullness by combing brows upward, filling in with color. Refer again to the Daily Makeup Techniques in Chapter Four to find out the best way to find your brow "bald spots" and fill them in. And, as we said there, always use two different pencils to color your brows. As they begin to lighten, blonde/gray or blonde/light brown combinations will provide shading that is softer and less obvious than darker tones or a single shade.

zone three the eye area

Those with fuller faces will notice it first, but sooner or later *everybody's* upper lid begins to "droop." It becomes heavy-looking, hiding the natural contours of the crease. To add insult to injury, this thin, stretched skin wrinkles quite easily.

It's only natural that wrinkles would appear in this area; the upper lid is extremely active. We blink on the average of ten thousand times a day, and there is only a thin fatty layer to absorb the shock. Moreover, there are few oil glands to lubricate the lid, and the skin itself is extremely thin (less than one millimeter thick).

So, before you begin any makeup, it is very important that this skin be properly nourished and hydrated. And for this, you go to the "specialists," products formulated specifically for the eye area. Eye restorers, which usually come in a gel or a light liquid emulsion, are less greasy and less rich than facial creams, which can cause puffiness if placed beyond the orbital bone. Once you've found the formulation that feels right for your eyes, use it twice a day, after cleansing your skin at night and before you do your makeup in the morning. You'll find that its "plumping" effect smoothes the surface of the skin for better makeup application.

quick fix
Stroke your eye shadow brush across an ice cube before dipping it into powder shadow. "Cold" shadow glides on better.

When you're ready to do your lid makeup, pamper and soothe your eyes a bit with cotton pads that have been soaked in ice water or chamomile tea. Rest these on your eyes for a few minutes, and you'll accomplish a lot. Any swelling will recede a little, and the skin will become more receptive to holding color. Eye shadow will glide on easier, stay on longer.

Next, you may wish to fortify the lid with a special eyelid base. Very light in texture, this base will hide apparent veins, smooth the shadows caused by wrinkles, and give the lids a healthy, unified skin tone. And if you don't like adding color to your lids, this is a good alternative to shadow, giving a nice nuance to the skin.

When you do choose to use color on the lids, think in terms of giving your eyes a "lift" of color and light. Avoid shades that are too dark or too obvious. They're never going to "sculpt" your lid back into shape, anyway—they're only going to draw more attention to it! Nor will it do you a bit of good to open your eyes wide, find the natural lid crease, and use a dark shadow where the separation between your brow bone and lid *used* to be. When your eye relaxes, your shadowing effort will disappear into the fold. Worse yet, your body heat will make it smudge every time you blink your eye.

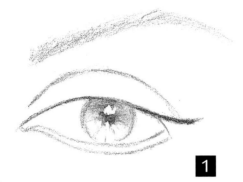

■ Droopy eyes can be minimized by sweeping upward with a thin line of eyeliner (1). Apply shadow at crease, blending upward, not extending below upward sweep of eyeliner (2). Follow the same parallel underneath the lower lash line, drawing a line that sweeps upward, without meeting the top line. On the upper lashes, apply mascara only to the place where the line begins to turn upward (3).

If your lids have become extremely droopy, use a very light touch with your mascara as well. A thick, dark veil of lashes only makes the eye area look heavier. However, lashes do thin with age, so you can't ignore them altogether. Apply the first two coats of mascara to the tips only (the thinnest part of the lash). Comb out to separate and let dry. Drying between coats makes the lashes look thicker, without building up clumpy clots. Sweep mascara from the roots to the tips only for your final coat.

Give lower lashes only one coat; making this area too dark only accentuates the darkness below the eye. Also, consider using a brown or charcoal gray mascara instead of black if the skin around the eyes is highly wrinkled. These shades are much more softening than black.

One word of warning: The eye will be drawn to every place you put color. It's like a little sign saying "Look at me." So choose very subtle, very nat-ural-looking shades, and never place them any-where *near* a spot that is badly wrinkled. If your eyes end in a web of crow's feet, for instance, never extend your shadow color out that far.

In the case of severe lid wrinkling, you may wish to dispense with color shadow altogether. Con-centrate, instead, on defining or correcting the shape of the eye by lining just at the base of the lashes. Start at the center of the lid and extend

■ **The best subterfuge for a heavy lid is a little touch of shadow just at the outside corner of the eyes, within your ascending eye parallels (1). Apply from the outside in-ward, with the heaviest emphasis just at the outer edge (2). A subtle taupe or smokey gray will add natural contour and a bit of depth, plus it will draw attention to the outer corner, away from the heaviest part of the lid. Avoid plac-ing a sweep of highlighter horizontally under the brow bone. Instead, for a natural glow, place a touch of blush just at the outside edge, under the brow bone, and blend it into the shadow. This, again, puts emphasis on the outer corner and gives the eyes a healthy "lift" (3).**

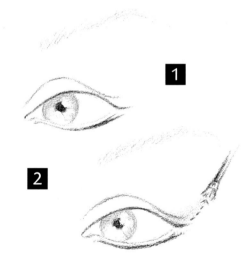

the line outward, along your parallels, thickening the line gradually. Unless your eyes are extremely wide set, do not line the lid from the center toward your nose, as this will only compound a natural darkness. Use the "roll-down" method of lining the eyes described in Chapter Four, and you won't have to worry about drawing a thin, precise line. And do use a gray, light brown, or navy blue shade, rather than black.

You can contour the shape of the eye with a line underneath the lower lid as well. Just remember to keep any line you draw here parallel to the ascending line of your brow. To reduce the obvious "lined" effect, take a flat brush, dip it in colorless, loose face powder, and brush it across the line to blend. Now your eyes have beautiful definition, without emphasizing the contours of a less-than-smooth lid.

■ **Deep-set eyes can be brought out by ignoring the natural crease and placing a darker sweep of shadow just *above* it. Apply a lighter shadow from the crease down to the lash line, covering the rest of the lid. Add a highlight under the brow bone. Line the eyes lightly, just at the base of the lashes.**

■ **Reduce the effect of bulging eyes by covering the lid with a soft, dark shadow (smoky gray or brown), extending it above the natural crease. Use a highlight shadow only under the arch of your brows. Add more interest to the underlash area with a soft line of color.**

zone four under-eye pouches

The under-eye area is very quick to show signs of aging. It is vulnerable to water retention, loss of elasticity, nasal and sinus congestion, even the dryness in the air, all of which contribute daily to wrinkling, sagging, and pouching.

An under-eye "bag" is really multidimensional. First, there is the pouch created when fat and water accumulate there, but because it bulges outward, it creates a surrounding hollow—the dark "circle" effect. So it's really a double whammy that can't be contoured away in a single concealing step. Successful subterfuge also takes a very precise highlighter application, so take your time. You don't want to emphasize the pouch or deepen the shadows in the hollow!

To make the bag less apparent, first chill the area with an icy cotton pad. This refreshes the skin, reduces puffiness, and allows products to glide on without dragging on tender skin. Next, apply your normal base. All correcting is done on top of, not underneath, foundation. Now apply base one shade darker *only* to the protruding pouches. Finally, use a small, angled brush to apply concealer only in the hollows. Take this lighter shade right to the inside corner of your eye, where there is often a bluish shadow.

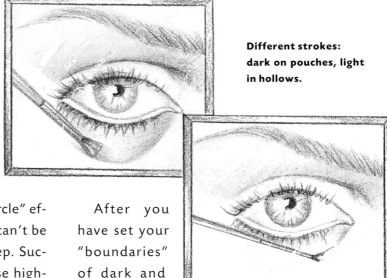

Different strokes: dark on pouches, light in hollows.

After you have set your "boundaries" of dark and light, tap your index finger all around the area to unify the shading and avoid giving the impression of obvious artwork. Nothing looks older than pale half-moons under the eyes! Powder helps to blend everything to a sheer, natural transparency with the skin, but you must be careful. Loose powder has a way of collecting inside ridges. So brush it on *lightly* with a big, fluffy brush, then wrap a tissue around your index finger and blot gently. (To avoid smearing the two shades together, try this trick: Wrap a tissue around your left index finger and dab at the darker colors; wrap a tissue around your right index finger and go at the lighter shades.)

zone five
cheeks and naso-labial area

es with concealer. Saturate a small brush with it and apply just inside the ridge. But that's it. Don't try to lighten or color cheek wrinkling. Avoid applying blush to these wrinkles, but if you must use it, be very sure to employ the tissue-wrap trick mentioned above to remove all excess color from the ridges. Then dust with a fluffy, clean, powder-free brush. Do this religiously. Powdery cheeks and dusty laugh lines simply make a face look old, whether it is or not!

The area that gives mobility and expression to the center of your face can suddenly "crumble" into a mass of wrinkles. Skin can lose its resiliency and change its texture, trapping makeup and color in the most unnatural places. The best thing to do when applying makeup is: Forget the furrows! Of course, you will want to lighten any deep "laugh line" creas-

quick fix

Keep a loose, colorless, transparent powder near your blusher products—and use it! This crucial second step softens the color and blends the edges.

lip fixers

■ Remember, a full, rounded shape is younger; flat, thin lips are harsh and strict. To find the ideal width for your lips, stare straight ahead into a mirror. Draw an imaginary line from the inner curve of the iris, down the cheeks to the lips. Anything that extends or droops beyond this point should simply not be colored.

■ If the area between the tip of your nose and the top of your lip seems to have shortened, it could be because the cartilage of your nose "settles" a little with age. Narrow your upper lip slightly by outlining just inside the natural line and filling in with color.

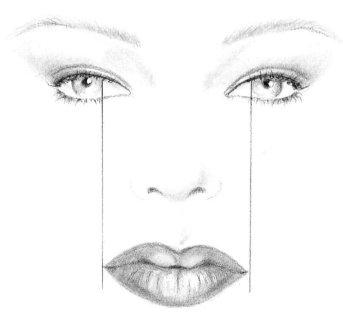

■ Base makes a good "adhesive" for lip color. Cover you lips completely with it. Or dip your lip brush into base, and outline around the edge of your lips after you've applied your lipstick. Powder over. This will form a barrier to hold color in, keep it from bleeding.

■ Lips that turn down at the end can be "lifted" by extending the lower lip and bringing the line slightly upward, going just a bit above the upper lip corner. Extend the upper lip to meet this line. Never take color down into the crease! Powder the pencil outline to soften and set it, then fill in with lipstick.

■ Wrinkly lips need the finish of a color-rich moisturizing lipstick to diffuse the light and soften creases. A matte lipstick just can't do that; it absorbs light and makes dry lips look even drier. Apply a rich, lustrous (not shiny) color and never powder over.

■ Puckered lips create such an uneven surface that lipstick often "skips" if you don't stretch your lips out between your second and third fingers while applying color. Line the ridge of your lips all around with a nongreasy pencil, or base, powder over, and apply lipstick just inside the line.

■ A clear, pink-based lip color is always more attractive as skin sallows. It makes the teeth look whiter and the whole face look rosier. But don't go for flaming fuchsia! A softer shade always looks younger than a brighter one.

zone six chin/jaw/neck

As this area becomes heavier, saggier, you may want to try subtle contouring, but only if you're comfortable with makeup. If your makeup is very sheer everyplace else, contouring the lower portion of your face will be much too obvious.

A smooth chin line goes into natural shadow gradually, with the deepest shadows falling just under the ears. To counteract the appearance of a wrinkled, jowly chin line, you'll want to start contouring at the center point, placing base a shade deeper under the point of the chin, and *lightening* toward the ears.

Resist the temptation to darken everything you don't like. You can't cover up wrinkles that way! In fact, if you have three too many chin lines, don't even attempt contouring. You simply can't make them disappear. The same is true for multiple horizontal lines around the neck, the so-called "necklace of Venus." Better to hide it with a scarf or a turtleneck. If you contour every crease, you'll end up with a striped neck!

zone seven the hands

Nothing reveals a woman's age more assuredly than her hands. Knuckles become more prominent and often gnarled with arthritis; the skin loosens and becomes crepey; and those dreaded "liver spots" make the skin look splotchy and discolored. But there are ways to deal with this.

For starters, shield the skin of your hands from the sun. Always and every day. The skin there is very thin, and brown spots multiply like polka dots without SPF protection! Wear gloves while gardening, and find a good hand cream with built-in sunblock protection to use daily. The spots will lighten naturally without repeated sun exposure, although they still may be obvious on pale, winter skin.

Special bleaching creams, containing mild concentrations of hydroquinone, can be obtained without prescription and will also help to fade spots. However, if you want more serious treatment, you'll have to use higher levels of hydroquinone, combined with Retin-A or glycolic acid peels to promote exfoliation and lighten age spots. More extreme forms of treatment include dermabrasion and laser surgery to eliminate broken capillaries.

Can anything be done to "plump up" dry, crinkled skin and surface lines? Some dermatologists will inject collagen or fat, taken from the buttocks to minimize rejection, if veins, tendons, and bones are seriously exposed. Before things get to that point, though, it's better to keep your hands well-moisturized and protected with daily conditioning and proper care.

Every vulnerable age zone has its own deconstruction schedule, and the clock starts ticking on some sooner than others. It has to do with sun exposure, weight loss or gain, general skin tone and fitness, and the inescapable predilections of heredity. But there's no need to fret when a sudden pouch or pucker appears, as long as you know a few trompe l'oeil tricks. Remember, an age zone never has to be a war zone.

changing beauty
updating your palette and beauty focus

chapter 7

Until recently, "showing" your age was never considered a good thing. Today it can be, as long as what shows is the security of knowing exactly who you are and liking it. Being happy with yourself is being beautiful. If the object of all these efforts is to accommodate a changing facial structure and maximize what you've got going for you, that's fine. If you're searching for a way to look younger, you'll lose what could be your most beautiful years. Younger isn't better. *Better* is better.

For each age, there is an approach to beauty. It's not determined by the calendar—you may look forty at fifty—but it is determined by the total harmony of your facial structure, your skin condition, your coloring. Finding the palette that enhances changing skin tones and hair color is far better than staying with long-loved shades. The same thing is true about makeup emphasis. Techniques that worked remarkably well in your thirties may seem as outdated on your face a decade later as the hairstyle you wore in high school. Knowing when, where, and how to make changes is what ageless beauty is all about.

Tips for Looking Ten Years Better

Not ten years younger. Ten years *better,* whatever your age. A lot has to do with attitude, of course. A positive approach to beauty maintenance can work wonders. Keep up with yourself, your body, your life-style. Make changes when necessary. If disability interferes with rigorous workouts, don't give up. Substitute brisk walks, swimming or water exercises, armchair isometrics. Muscle tone and good circulation go a long way to giving you a beautiful glow.

There are always very simple "up" things you can do to look and feel ten years better. The trick is to do them!

Polish Up

Keep your skin in the best possible condition with proper treatment. Nourish it with the best formulations you can afford, care for it with a daily regimen. And select your makeup by texture, for adequate coverage, minimal congestion. Look for lighter textures, but not transparency. Some opacity helps skin tones that are becoming uneven.

Ease Up

Soften your colors, avoid hard-edged lines and obvious contouring. Intensify your makeup as the day goes on rather than overloading your skin with a heavy-handed morning application. And, after applying each product, dab a dry sponge everywhere to remove excess and soften.

Perk Up

Lift the lines of your face with a well-shaped "frame." Treat your hair to a shorter, more modern style. Add a soft fringe of bangs (not a hard, straight-across cut) to hide forehead furrows, receding hairlines, thinning brows. Try the boost of a more cheerful hair color. At a certain age, many women want "wash and wear" hair, so they cut it, perm it, and forget it. Unfortunately, they become forgettable, too! A tight "dandelion" cap of gray frizz does nothing to soften or complement a face.

Shape Up

Remember, sags and bags aren't reserved for your face alone! Do what you can to ensure upper-arm tone and a firm abdomen, buttocks, and thighs. Take ten deep breaths as often as you can. You'll walk better, stand better, feel better

Facing Up to Changes
New Life-style Choices

As you have no doubt gathered by now, the entire aging process is a long, gradual transition that encompasses every facet of your being. Your face is changing, your skin is changing, your hormones are changing, even the very cells that travel through your body are changing. You have little control over most of these processes. But there are other changes—in your life, in the choices you make, in your habits—that can affect your looks dramatically. You may put on weight or lose it. You may redefine your face with glasses or suddenly switch to contacts. And, most common to those of retirement age, you may change your life-style, move to a different climate, and need a simpler beauty routine.

Such change can be stimulating, exciting and challenging. But if you don't learn to accommodate life changes with new beauty techniques you'll look older, out of synch with the changes around you. For instance, if your face becomes fuller or thinner, refer again to the face-shaping techniques in Chapter Five, choosing those that work for the shape your face is *now*—not what it once was. If your face has become too thin, all the makeup sculpting in the world won't do you as much good as gaining a few pounds. The thinner you are, the more accentuated the vertical lines of your face will be, which can contribute to a sunken, haggard appearance.

The Perfect Palette Principle

If you look at the way the character of your face, the structure of your face, and the coloring of your face, eyes, and hair interact with one another, you'll find what makes you uniquely you. Color is a crucial part of this equation. It must shade and accentuate softly in order to give natural contour and definition. When accent colors are chosen from your personal palette, they unify everything. If a certain color doesn't harmonize with your skin tone, hair color, and the other colors of your cosmetics, it will go "tilt."

Balance Skin and Hair

To find your own personal palette, start with your hair color, the way it is now. This is what gives an immediate impression; moreover, it acts as a frame for your face. Next, examine your skin tone. If the underlying tone (yellow or blue) doesn't work with your hair color, you'll appear sallower or paler than you're used to. Correct this first by either neutralizing the yellow or bluish cast with your base, or by changing your hair color to a shade with less gold, red, or burgundy in it. If you opt for the latter, discuss your options with a professional hair colorist.

Once hair color and complexion are brought into a beautiful balance, each underlying tone complementing the other, you have the foundation for creating a perfect palette. On the next pages, you'll find palettes for a variety of skin tones and hair colors. One should be yours.

One note: Establishing your personal palette isn't about locking you into a system of color. Some women have allowed their choices to be limited by insisting they can only wear "cool" tones or "warm" tones. Nonsense. If you coordinate color to maintain a harmony with your natural coloring, you can wear many different shades beautifully.

chestnut hair/ olive skin

A rich, warm hair color looks wonderful against paler skin (think of Snow White). Unfortunately, those born with Mediterranean coloring often have a sallow tone to their skin. From opposite palettes, the contrast is not complementary. Dark hair can tend to "draw" color from a sallow complexion.

The Strategy

- **Neutralize sallow undertones!**
- **Pink nuances in foundation, blusher, lip color**
- **Taupes or grayish browns for eyelids, mascara, eye pencils**
- **Bois de rose or slightly browned reds for lips**

fair hair/ fair skin

Many natural childhood-blond locks fade to light brown before they turn gray! If you choose to color-boost your hair, give a boost to your makeup palette, too. Play with color; add definition. If everything becomes too pale or too neutral in tone, you'll fade away!

The Strategy

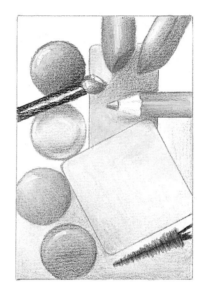

- **Enliven your face with color!**
- **Beige and brown shadows, lavender, gold**
- **Mascara and eye pencils in a soft nut brown, olive green, violet**
- **Transparent pink blush**
- **Reddish brown or golden pink lip color**

black hair/ sallow skin

Full-strength, unequivocal hair color calls attention to itself, whether it's black, red, blond or white. Your makeup is left to compete or disappear. One word of caution: There's a fine line between an equally strong palette, and one that's overpowering.

The Strategy

- **Add *subtle* drama!**
- **Eyes in mauves, lilac, grays, or black**
- **A sharp-edged pink for blush**
- **Black or navy mascara and eye pencils**
- **Luminous, strong reds or pinks for lips**

red hair/pale skin

Women born with the natural vibrancy of red hair may go through life soft-pedaling make-up, and that's a mistake. Your face needs to live up to your hair. Because redheads' complexions often tend to be paler and more delicate, they need to be softly, but subtly, warmed. Earthy neutrals are to your advantage.

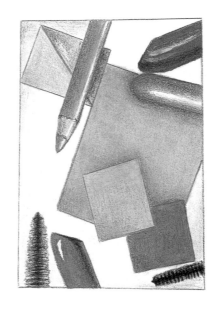

The Strategy

- **Play it soft with warmed pastels!**
- **Soft greens, warm beiges for eyes, highlighted with gold**
- **Dark brown, auburn mascaras and eye pencils**
- **Coral or coral beige for cheeks, highlighted with gold**
- **Browned reds or corals for lips**

107

salt-and-pepper hair/dark skin

Women with dark complexions may think that natural pigmentation is all they need as they get older. Sadly, this is not so. Your skin can turn ashen and dull. If your hair begins to lighten, it only compounds the problem. Now is the time to try more interesting colors, more emphatic combinations.

The Strategy

- **Heighten the impact with bolder strokes!**
- **Taupey charcoals, golds for eyelids**
- **Black mascara, charcoal and lavender eye pencils**
- **Bronzed reds, natural ambers for cheeks**
- **Deep burgundy or warmed copper lip color**

gray hair/pale skin

White hair is a definitive color; gray hair isn't. It's actually a composite of many colors: your natural "pre-gray" shades, yellows, or lavender-blues. Ignore the indecisive cues your hair sends you and let your face be the focal point. Keep makeup fresh, light, and unified, with skin-brightening tones.

The Strategy

- Add prettiness with pink-based tones!
- Pastel lavenders, pinks, soft blues for eyelids
- Softly smudged black or gray pencil, black or vibrant violet mascara
- Pale pink cheeks, soft blued pink lip color

Life Plan for Beauty

The first day of a new decade may be cause for celebration for some, despair for others. However you are feeling inwardly, why not celebrate these milestones outwardly with a new approach to beauty? Let each ten years provide a new focus, a different point of view, for your beauty, and you'll keep up to date with your face.

Following are appropriate makeup strategies for the thirties, forties, fifties, and sixties. These are not hard-and-fast rules to be observed the very morning of your birthday. If you still look thirty-something on your fortieth birthday, wait until you catch up with your chronology. Use this information only as a guideline to changing beauty. You'll know when it's time to try something new.

the threshhold thirties

The thirties is a decade of major change for many women. Families are started or growing, careers are escalating, time is in short supply. And so there is a temptation to cling to a beauty routine that was simpler, easier, and successful all through the twenties. That's the danger. If you don't update your face, you'll end up looking like an overaged teenager! You should develop a certain sophistication to your look now, project a more polished image, even if you prefer a natural style.

Not every woman will want—or need—full foundation coverage; if your skin is healthy and glowing, a moisturizer plus powder is enough to smooth and substantiate skin tone. If you prefer the effect of a base, use a light moisturizer first, follow with an oil-free base, and powder over. Work with two to three eyeshadow shades—never one—to define the eyes. (Surrounding the eye with a single shade will appear too harsh against a minimal makeup.) Blend these tones, lightest to deepest (inside to outside) to create a subtle, rounded-lid effect. You can stay with a palette of neutral tones, or choose something more dramatic in the blue, mauve, or green families, depending on your wardrobe choices. Use blusher (at this point, brighter is nicer) to highlight cheekbones, browbone, temple and chinline, again giving the face curve and definition. And now's the time to let your lips shine! Shape your mouth with a lipliner pencil; fill in with a bright burst of color; add a touch of gloss. All of these touches will lend stature and importance to your face, to go along with all that you've become . . . all that you're becoming.

the fortunate forties

A famous New York plastic surgeon calls the forties "the unkindest decade," simply because it's the time most women are first confronted with obvious signs of aging. While these can come as a shock, there's no reason to run for cover. In fact, your features are now at their most feminine, their most powerful, so play them up for all they're worth!

This is the time to let your eyes grab all the attention. Give them more expression for daytime, more drama for night, but do it in a new way. Instead of playing tricks with color, concentrate on defining the *shape* of the eye. The contour will start to soften and change as time goes by, so clarify it now with a deeper color in the eyelid crease, a sharper line around the edges of the eye, and a good highlight on the brow bone. Use mascara to its full advantage, separating and shaping the lashes with each stroke. And don't forget that a well-defined eyebrow draws all eyes to you!

If you've been using high-gloss lipsticks, now is the time to switch to rich, moisturizing ones. They'll give you enough shine, *and* they'll help keep your lips soft and young. Use blush as liberally as you like, but stick to natural "blush" shades. Avoid browns or earth tones; your skin tone may be just starting to turn a bit sallow. And, if you've ever wanted to try an angular, modern hairstyle, don't save it for the future; do it now while your face shape and features are still well-defined.

the intriguing fifties

Many women find that their fifties is their time to shine. Responsibilities change, insecurities seem to melt away, and a new attractiveness takes over. The danger is, if your self-confidence is at an all-time high, you may think you can get away with anything. You can't. This is the time when makeup can accentuate every little problem. As your features begin to soften, it's the perfect time to begin little "lifting" techniques. Concentrate color away from the center of your face. Eye shadow should be darker at the outer corner of the eye. Eyebrows should be more defined along the descending line of the arch. Place the arch slightly off-center, and lift the line up and away from the eye.

You can use stronger colors of blush and lipstick, carefully shaping the lips to make them a very nice focal point for the face. Add a bit of blush at the jawline to define the chin. The object is to use color to draw attention away from obvious lines and creases.

the simplified sixties

This is a time when the adage "Less is more" truly comes into play. And it may be the first time in your life that a simpler strategy really works for you. Switch to matte textures (if you haven't already done so), and add a soft glow with a light finish of translucent powder.

Concentrate again on your eyes, defining their shape with light—never clumpy—mascara. Sweep a taupe or light brown eye shadow shade from lash to crease to take away puffiness and carve out a contour. Add a healthy peachy highlight just at the brow bone if you want a little more accent.

Use a light hand with blush, sweeping it away from under-eye wrinkling, and along the jawbone.

For special problems like spidery veins or brown spots, dip a small eyeliner blush into a lighter, pink-toned base and trace the discoloration exactly, applying it over your base. If you choose to use a concealer, don't dab it on randomly with your finger; you'll cover too much area. Instead, mix the concealer with a little moisturizer first and apply it with your eyeliner brush. For any red splotches or veins, invest in a special base or concealer that has some green in it. This really gets the red out! Remember to always unify these "touch-ups" by lightly repowdering after application.

You'll want to pay more attention to your lips now, without making them the focal point of your face. Use two pencils to define the shape and keep lipstick from bleeding: a light, brownish one to correct the lip's shape, a pencil close to the color of your lipstick to outline just inside the correcting line. (See Chapter Four for more lip-lining tricks.) Keep lips naturally attractive with clear, fresh, unflashy colors.

New Places, New Faces

Rethink every product you use when you're making a move. Don't automatically pack up the old standbys. A difference in the chemical composition of the water you cleanse with; a difference in your proximity to the sun; a difference in daily habits; a difference in the very air that surrounds you—any of these may require a change in the way you care for your skin and what you choose to put on your face. Ignore the environment, and your first appointment in your new location may be with a dermatologist! Your skin is simply going to act up if the products aren't right for the setting.

If a change in your environment has increased the humidity in the air, you may need to adjust products to the new moisture balance of your skin. Reconsider your moisturizer, your base, and the formulation of other accent color cosmetics. Remember, just as cool, dry weather can rob skin of moisture, causing it to lose its flexibility, higher humidity levels can often cause products to "slip" off the skin. Moisturizers containing humectants (attracting whatever moisture is in the air) may be fine for dry, windy, cold climates, but totally unnecessary where the air naturally bathes the skin with moisture. Oil-based makeups may also be too greasy for warmer climes, unless your skin is excessively dry.

Keep in mind, however, that sun accentuates the drying effects of the air, increasing actinic aging (wrinkles, brown spots) in *every* climate. If you've moved to cooler climes, heavier formulations, double coats of moisturizers, and waxy, skin-coating products all form additional protective barriers from the sun; using products with sunscreening agents effectively increases your safety shield.

Taking a Look at Glasses

By the mid-forties, the muscles that help the eye focus become less elastic, and corrective lenses may become essential. And what a difference they make in your face! Even if you've worn glasses all your life, you've most likely changed your frames through the years, as both fashion—and your face—have changed. Although you may think you know by now which frame shapes are the most flattering to you, take the time to try on those you never would have considered ten or fifteen years ago. Remember, the structure of your face is changing; the support system of your cheekbones is shifting; your eyebrows and hair may be lightening; your lips may appear thinner or lower. A new frame shape or color may balance your whole face better.

If you're new to wearing glasses, don't despair! They're not going to detract from your beauty one bit. In fact, quite the opposite may be true. Well-chosen frames can add definition, focus, and personality to a face. The best advice is to go into frame selection with your eyes—and mind—open!

Whether you're buying replacement frames or

first-time glasses, the most important consideration is your brow line. Your frames must never compete with it. The ideal shape will correspond perfectly with the gentle rounding of your brow. If you can't find frames that are perfectly harmonious, it is better to select slightly squared-off tops which leave the brows apparent, without causing a "double brow" effect.

The size of the frame is always a personal decision; it has to feel good on the face. In general, it is better to select the largest lenses your face can support. It's less disruptive to see the whole eye—wrinkles and all—than to cut off the most expressive part of your face with heavy, horizontal lines.

Many women who need corrective lenses find it difficult to put on eye makeup. It's almost impossible to apply with glasses on, just as impossible with glasses off! Fortunately, there are ways around this problem. Flip-up makeup glasses allow you to lift one hinged lens up at a time and still see with the other eye. And there are always large magnifying mirrors. Choose one that shows your entire face. With these, there's simply no need to squint or play hit-and-miss around your eyes!

The question is, do you need makeup behind glasses? The answer is, emphatically—yes! First of all, glasses can create shadows around your eyes and magnify under-eye wrinkles. It's important to lighten the entire area with a base that's a shade lighter than your normal color. Frames can also darken the inner corner of the eye, so you don't want to draw attention there. Begin all shadowing or eye-lining at the outside corner, and apply only to the outer quarter of the lid.

Be cautious in how you use color shadow; subtle gradations don't register as well when you wear glasses, and iridescence looks horrible when magnified by corrective lenses. Concentrate, instead, on defining and intensifying the shape of your eye by lining just above and below the lash line, always moving color to the lash line with an applicator swab or small brush. You can exaggerate these lines if you are nearsighted because your lenses will reduce everything. Add a touch of blush to the lids to add eye-brightening color, but then don't use too much blush on your cheeks. Believe it or not, blush can clash with the color of your frames or, at the very least, compete with them.

Spectacle wearers can use mascara, but be careful. Don't choose extra-fiber lengthening formulations, which can flake onto the lenses. Apply mascara with light strokes, and use a lash comb to separate lashes in between coats. It's more important to have a clean look than a smudgy, smoky effect. Behind lenses, that only translates as messy.

Time to Simplify

Every so often it's a good idea to take stock of your beauty routine. You may find that your beauty style is far too complicated for the way you live now. Perhaps you've left a job and no longer feel the need for an executive style. Perhaps you've moved to a warm climate and lead a very casual, outdoor-oriented life. Perhaps you've simply decided to uncomplicate your life.

At this stage of the game, some women give up on beauty altogether, but there's no need to, when maintaining any attractive appearance is as easy as one, two, three.

One: Cleanse. Keep your skin in glowing condition. This may mean increasing your schedule of professional care, but your skin needs it now more than ever. Treat yourself to monthly facials, exfoliating masks, mineral treatments. Guard against sun damage daily and pamper your skin with light, restorative lotions designed to help "boost" the moisture-bonding effects of your moisturizer. Pay particular attention to the eye area, making use of special products formulated for this skin alone. And never "retire" from proper skin maintenance; cleanse it and treat it twice a day.

Two: Prepare. Protect your skin by day with a light, sunscreen-formulated base. If you omit this, you'll have to do that much more to compensate for the damaging effects of the sun! Base is your quickest beauty ally; it unifies the complexion, covers brown spots, corrects sallowness, and shields the skin from danger—all in one simple application. Apply a light, translucent powder with a damp sponge to "set" your makeup to avoid having a powdery look.

quick fix

For perfect "frame-ups," balance the focus on the eyes with a richly colored mouth.

Your makeup will stay in place the whole day, and it will have taken you two minutes.

Three: Finish. Adding accent colors is a matter of choice (although lipstick is *always* a must; pale, dry lips are old lips). You may save the colors for evening, perhaps you won't go out in broad daylight without them. But the whole procedure can be very simple.

For a quick eye pickup, day or night, touch your blush brush to your lids to give them a healthy color. Then mix a drop of moisturizer with concealer and dab only on dark shadows. Never resort to circling your eyes quickly with white or a too-light concealer. It gives a ghoulish effect! Fortunately, cosmetic companies are now matching concealer shades to their bases or to a wider range of skin tones—beyond Light, Medium, and Dark. Look for them.

Accentuating thinning lashes with mascara can sometimes make them look scrawnier. Instead, outline the eye with a neutral pencil (charcoal gray, brown, taupe), then push the color down to the lash line with a brush. The effect makes your lashes look fuller, without coating them with color. You might also try the tips-to-roots technique to make thin lashes look fuller, applying your first coat only to the tips, letting them dry, then following up with a sweep from roots to tips. Finally, if your lashes are really hopeless and you don't want to be bothered with them, consider having them professionally dyed. This procedure not only darkens lashes, it actually makes the lash hair thicker.

For your blush, choose a very natural pink or coral color; stay away from brown, apricot, and anything iridescent. Respect the undertone of your skin with your lipstick shade. Don't think pink if you have sallow coloring; don't go toward orange or rust if your skin has a pink or slightly blue cast.

Rex's Seven Steps for Taking the Fatigue out of Your Face

Fatigue can add years to your appearance. Your skin loses a bit of its natural elasticity, causing your complexion to become sallow, muddy, gray. Want a quick pickup? Try the following:

1. Stay away from yellow or brown-based makeup shades. Anything that says tawny, honey, or bisque is not for you today. Use a base with an underlying rose tone.

2. If you don't get along well with blue-based pinks, change your blush from peach or apricot to a clear coral. If you can think pink, by all means, leave the peaches behind and go for a rosy blusher.

3. Do not apply any bronzing products. Tan doesn't make you look healthy, blush does. You want to enhance your skin with color, not darken it.

4. Lighten up on eye makeup; heavy, dark rings of mascara will only make your eyes look tired. If the whites of your eyes are reddened or slightly yellow, add a rim of pale blue color just at the base of the lashes.

5. Sweep a pink shadow along the top of your brow bone, just under your eyebrow, to make eyes look more alert, fresher.

6. Skip the powder for today. It's only going to trap the light, when what you really need is more glow.

7. See red. A pale mouth makes you look a little washed out. A bright red mouth degrays a mixed complexion and illuminates the skin. The good thing about red is, you don't need to add a lot of color anyplace else; it takes over. While you're at it, this might just be the day to bring out that red suit!

A   C h a n g e   f o r   t h e   B e t t e r

No matter how your life and your looks may change, welcome the difference. You can't ignore some changes; you can't fight others. The thing to do is accept change for what it is, and learn how to make the most of it. There are things you can do to feel better and look better during this natural evolution. There are ways to adapt your beauty to your new lifestyle, your new environment. A graceful break with the past is only possible if your philosophy, your approach to your own well-being, changes right along with everything else!

plastic surgery

a plus or a pain?

chapter 8

There may come a time when you are considering making corrections that go beyond base and blush. The decision to surgically alter your features in any way is never an easy one to make. Those who know you best may be able to advise you, but in the end, only you can make the choice. Because surgery has become an option for more and more women, we must consider it here. These chapters are intended to provide you with information, not recommendations! Before you contemplate *any* surgical alternative, collect all the information you can, talk to one or more surgeons experienced in these cosmetic procedures, and decide what's best for you.

Statistics show that an increasing number of people—both men and women—are "having something done" to soften signs of aging. According to the American Society of Plastic and Reconstructive Surgeons, procedures performed to lift, augment, inject, sculpt, and redefine body contours increased 69 percent from 1981 to 1990.

These fall into the category of aesthetic or cosmetic surgery. (Reconstructive surgery, to correct disfigurement from injury, disease, or birth defects, is another matter altogether.)

Although many aesthetic procedures do not involve a scalpel, you must keep in mind that many do create a trauma and a wound, and they must be as seriously considered as any surgery. As Dr. John Anton, chief of Plastic Surgery at Southampton Hospital, puts it, "Surgery means inducing an injured state in a controlled fashion, so the results, when healed, will presumably be better." And therein lies the essence of cosmetic surgery's unpredictability. The ultimate success of any procedure depends as much on your own healing ability as it does on the skill of the surgeon you select.

Still, plastic surgery has come into the mainstream as well as out of the closet. It's not a big secret anymore. The names of top surgeons are as eagerly traded as good hairdressers or therapists. In fact, word of mouth is now the best referral a surgeon can hope for. Perhaps this is because men and women no longer wait until nature has done its worst to seek surgery. They begin earlier, seeing it as an anti-aging strategy, right up there along with body toning and proper diet. In 1990, The ASPRS revealed that 57 percent of dermabrasion procedures were performed on patients between the ages of nineteen and thirty-four, the same age range that accounted for 44 percent of liposuctions and 57 percent of nose reshaping. In the thir-

ty-five to fifty age category, 28 percent of chemical peels were performed, 54 percent of all collagen injections, 44 percent of all eyelid surgery, 53 percent of fat injections, 38 percent of forehead lifts, 45 percent of Retin-A treatments, and 64 percent of tummy tucks. Only face-lifts show a majority of patients (59 percent) in the fifty-one to sixty-four age range, and today many surgeons would say that's too old, advising patients to undergo the surgery earlier, when skin tissue has more resiliency. As Dr. Michael Evan Sachs, the director of research in the Division of Facial Plastic and Reconstructive Surgery, New York Eye and Ear Infirmary/New York Medical College, states, "You can't suddenly go into a gym at 65 and expect great results. Why would you expect perfection if you wait too long to tone up your face?"

Sachs is among the surgeons who believe that a face-lift done in the early forties actually reinforces the tissues. With procedures that lift the total structural foundation, supporting ligaments become scarred, stronger, less apt to let fatty pouches bulge through.

When—and if—you choose to eliminate undesirable signs of aging is between you and your mirror. Notice when the facial contour of your face changes, when the nose begins to become longer and a little droopy, when the earlobes look longer, when loose folds of skin begin to collect under your chin. Can these be corrected? Yes. Should they be? That's a choice that is strictly up to you.

How to Choose a Surgeon

If you live in a major metropolitan area, chances are there are noted plastic surgeons who have become big-name superstars. Everybody talks about them. Everybody who is anybody goes to them. But very few fall into this rarified echelon, and even well-known surgeons don't always achieve perfect results. You can travel cross-country or cross-continent to these superstars, wait six months to two years for an appointment, or you can scout around for a less ballyhooed but equally well-qualified surgeon. One who may not pioneer news-making techniques, but performs the specialty you seek with skill and expertise.

Surprisingly, a plastic surgeon is not your only choice; many kinds of doctors perform plastic surgery today, including gynecologists, dermatologists, otolaryngologists, and ear, nose, and throat specialists. A general medical degree entitles doctors to practice any specialty they wish, regardless of formal training in that specialty. On the other hand, a plastic surgeon certified by the American Board of Plastic Surgery must complete an approved two-to-three-year residency specifically in plastic surgery after a three-to-five-year residency in general surgery. Only then is the doctor fully qualified to perform both aesthetic and reconstructive procedures.

How can you tell if your surgeon has met these standards? Board certification is an essential credential. But not all boards are created equal. Currently, there are nearly a dozen cosmetic and plastic surgery boards in the United States. Only one, the American Board of Plastic Surgery, is recognized by the American Board of Medical Specialties for plastic surgery. This is a good place to start for referrals (1-800-635-0635). Your library is another source of information. Consult the American Board of Medical Specialties' *Compendium of Certified Medical Specialists.* All board-certified specialists are listed by specialty and state.

Never choose a surgeon whose work you don't know—directly or indirectly. If you know of no other woman who has been a patient of this doctor, ask if you may contact two or three previous patients. If you are not given any names, consider another doctor immediately. You should have the opportunity to speak directly to other patients. This doesn't mean going to their homes to stare at their scars. A courteous, brief phone call will tell you all you need to know. Ask about the total experience, beyond the success of the surgery. Find out if the doctor was available to them after surgery, if he or she was helpful and understanding, what the postoperative treatment was like. Remember, you're making a very important commitment, both emotionally and financially, and you deserve a doctor who is committed to your care.

Every doctor knows that a prospective patient may consult with several surgeons before selecting one. You'd never have work done on your car or your home without doing the same. But don't turn your interview into an audition; it isn't a comfortable situation. Of course you are comparison shopping, but you don't have to be obvious about it. There is a certain consultation etiquette that, if observed, will lead to a much more gratifying interview—for both doctor and patient.

■ **Present yourself as you would for any interview—job, college, club, etc. Don't be too casual, don't be too nervous. Your best approach: serious, relaxed, and confident.**

■ **Do your homework first. Be as knowledgeable as you can about the procedure(s) you desire. A reasonable consultation time is fifteen to thirty minutes. Don't waste it by asking uninformed questions.**

■ **Know who you're talking to. You can check the doctor's credentials with the office manager, nurse, or medical directories. In addition to determining whether he or she has proper board certification, ask to see a curriculum vitae, find out where the doctor is published, what books he or she has written, what societies he or she belongs to. Medical schools, fellowships, professorships at teaching hospitals also indicate the caliber of the doctor. This you can learn on your own. If you take the time to ask about these things during a consultation, you're taking time away from your own questions.**

■ **Look around you. Be aware of the aesthetics of the office. It must be more than clean and neat. Surroundings suggest artistic sensibilities. And you *are* choosing an artist. You are also choosing a combination family doctor, superspecialist, and psychiatrist. So you have to be a bit of an analyst, too!**

■ **Be as definitive as you can. Never give a doctor carte blanche. It only says you don't know what you want; you haven't given the matter proper consideration. Ask: "What would you suggest to improve my nose?" or "What do you feel is the best procedure for these bags under my eyes?" Never ask: "What could you do for my face?"**

■ **Bring pictures of features you like, if you wish, but make sure the surgeon knows you are using them only as a reference point. They may help if you have trouble putting exactly what you are looking for into words. Pictures give the doctor something to go on, not a blueprint for your surgery.**

■ **Be honest. If you've had cosmetic surgery before, admit it. Discuss any problems that you feel occurred without being overly critical of previous experiences (unless they were obvious disasters!). The surgeon is going to be wary of "doctor hoppers."**

■ **Ask to see patient pre- and postsurgery shots. These will give you both an overview of what the doctor can accomplish, as well as the type of work he or she most likes to do.**

Many surgeons show a definite preference or skill for one type of procedure over another.

■ Feel comfortable that the doctor understands what you want. Ask specific questions: "What about the hump on my nose? Will you take it off or just leave it lower?"

■ Don't be afraid to ask about complications, risks, healing time. Let the doctor know if there are time constraints on your schedule: "I have to be back at my desk in a week," "I fly frequently; any danger of encouraging bleeding?" "How long will the bruising last?"

■ Discuss long-range aesthetic objectives. Don't feel pressured into doing "everything" all at once. Ask if the doctor can suggest a five-year plan, a ten-year plan. If a doctor steers you away from a moderate approach, steer away from the doctor!

■ Be frank about finances. Once the surgeon knows the extent of the procedures you are considering, he or she may give you a general "ballpark" cost during your initial interview. Follow up with the office or business manager to get the final tally, and make sure it includes all additional charges (anesthesiologist's fees, facility fees, etc—even if the surgery is performed in a doctor's office, there is usually an additional charge for the facility). It is a common practice for surgeons to require that all fees be paid in full prior to the surgery, often one week in advance. And most insurance companies will not reimburse you for cosmetic procedures, although some will cover hospital-related costs. To avoid the "taxi meter" charges of hospital stays, where every aspirin adds up, some hospitals today offer a flat fee for cosmetic surgery patients—payable ahead of time.

■ Feel comfortable. If, at the end of the consultation, you are impressed with the surgeon but didn't feel you had a good interview, call the office manager in a week or so and ask if you can come back for a follow-up. Some surgeons insist on a second interview, after you've had time to think things over, discuss them with your family, come up with new questions. Many do not charge for a repeat visit—but don't make a pest of yourself!

How a Surgeon Chooses You

It would be naive to think that you aren't being as carefully evaluated as the doctor at your consultation. You most definitely are. When you enter a surgeon's office, you are only a candidate for surgery. What goes on during the interview will determine whether or not the doctor considers taking you on as a patient. You will have to demonstrate that you have the right motivation and the right attitude.

There are countless, sometimes hidden, reasons why a person decides to have plastic surgery, and a doctor will very tactfully try to get at yours. A key question a surgeon might ask is "Why are you considering the procedure *now*?" If you're there because you're on the brink of divorce, a doctor has to consider misplaced animosity if your marriage goes right out with your wrinkles. If you've got your heart set on a nose or cheekbones that have nothing to do with your anatomy, ethnic background, or family heritage, the doctor should alert you to what is within the realm of physical possibility. If your expectations remain unrealistic, your eventual disappointment may mean trouble. If the doctor senses that you're a person who is never satisfied, he or she may decide not to even try. Without confidence, on both parts, neither one of you should take the next step.

What Can Be Done

Plastic surgery today is a lot different than it used to be. Even standard procedures, such as eyelid surgery (blepharoplasty), nose surgery (rhinoplasty), and face-lifts (rhytidectomy), have been noticeably refined to reduce scarring and give more natural, longer-lasting results. Gone is the masklike immobility and artificiality of too-perfect features. New techniques are continually being pioneered to respect both the underlying structure and natural contours of your face.

The ultimate objective of cosmetic surgery hasn't changed, however. Doctors are still dealing with the three factors that make faces look older: puffiness, sagging, and wrinkles. But just as there are various kinds of wrinkles, so there are various means of treating them. Fine, spidery wrinkles form a mosaic of tiny lines, especially at eye corners, lips, and chin. Etched into the skin by sun damage as well as natural aging, they cannot be removed by surgery alone. Deeper creases that extend with every passing year, especially from nose to mouth, across the forehead, and between the eyes, may be softened by a combination of techniques. Droopy folds of skin of the upper eyelids and around the jowl and neck area do need surgery to eliminate the stretch and sag caused by a loss of skin elasticity. Puffiness, on the other hand, that has not stretched delicate under-eye skin and weakened supporting ligaments beyond repair may be addressed without an incision at all.

Selecting a corrective technique that's going to do the most for you, with the least amount of damage, is a matter between you and your doctor. Keep in mind that your skin type, genetic makeup, and specific aging characteristics all must be considered. And, no matter how revolutionary or routine the procedure, a few wrinkles will always remain—and should. Without normal wrinkles to allow facial movement, you'll lose natural expression—the most beautiful asset of any face.

For Fine Lines ...

Nothing "erases" the tiniest wrinkles, but there are a number of remedies that can smooth them and give more consistency to the surface of your skin. Though not permanent, results can be extremely effective.

Collagen treatments Collagen can be injected directly into the areas where your own wrinkles and lines exist, raising these depressions to the level of the surrounding skin. The drawback is, the body absorbs it gradually, so treatment must be repeated every three to six months. Until recently, purified cow collagen (known as Zyderm® or Zyplast®) was the only substance used for this procedure, but it is not for everybody. Those with autoimmune diseases (including arthritis, lupus erythmatosis, and multiple sclerosis), a history of systemic allergic reaction, or a sensitivity to lidocaine (injected with the material for anesthetic purposes) cannot use it. And allergic reactions to the collagen itself can occur, even after previously successful injections. A very new procedure involves autogenous collagen, made from your own skin tissues. A graft is taken from the underarms or thighs, or during a face-lift or eye-lift. Collagen is extracted from the sample and frozen, and then injected over a period of months or years. With either method, initial puffiness around treated areas generally subsides within a few days as the collagen incorporates itself into your own skin.

Chemical Peels An effective procedure for the lines along the upper and lower lips, areas of excessive sun damage, and dark shadows under the eyes, chemical peels essentially destroy the top layer of skin, allowing new, unwrinkled skin to surface. A toxic solution is applied to a specific area, which irritates and reddens the skin. Eventually, it scabs and falls off. Some doctors apply tape after the procedure, which peels off the dead skin when it is removed. Changes in pigmentation often occur, as the new skin may be either lighter or darker than the original surface, and blotchiness can also result, especially in people with freckled skin. For this reason, doctors perform both peels and dermabrasion in symmetrical "aesthetic units," balancing pigmentation changes on both sides of a chin, lip, or cheek. Makeup is also a must, after healing, to even out skin tone. Chemical peels are best for smaller areas of the face; deep, full-face peels must involve cardiac monitoring, as they can cause irritability of the heart.

Dermabrasion Following the same principle as the chemical peel, dermabrasion involves "sanding" off surface skin with a small grinding wheel. This is done under either general or local anesthesia, and actually requires less healing time than a chemical peel, from ten to fourteen days. There is also less potential for pigmentation changes, although they can occur. When your skin returns to normal, acne scars, fine lines, sunspots, and enlarged blood vessels are smoothed away. But don't even think about going out in the sun for at least six months without a total block. The "new" skin is tender and highly susceptible to severe burning and permanent pigmentation change.

For Deeper Creases...

Forehead furrows and deep "laugh lines" are no laughing matter for some women. Although collagen injections may soften subtler grooves, you may want to consider more long-lasting techniques.

Autogenous Tissue Transfer (also known as Fat Injection)

Following a similar principle as that used in autogenous collagen injections, tissue from fatty areas of the body (saddlebag thighs, abdomen, or hips) is placed where it will do the most good—in deep naso-labial lines or frown furrows. These injections tend to be absorbed over a three-to-six-month period. Surgeons also may remove extra muscle tissue from underneath an eyelid during an eye-lift and thread it directly into wrinkles.

Threading A newer procedure involves placing surgical threads made of natural glycerine protein directly under the wrinkle line. In about six months, your body builds up its own natural collagen around the threads in the form of scar tissue, and the protein thread dissolves. Because this collagen replacement is your own, it lasts several years longer than artificial collagen injection, but it is as subject to natural aging as the rest of the collagen under your skin.

Tissue Clay Injections A protein-based powder, mixed with your own blood, forms a kind of natural "putty" which may be placed underneath the skin to plump up deeper wrinkles. Applied to resculpt bony areas, it acts like bone when it solidifies. Added to skin, it remains soft, retaining a fleshy nature. Over time, the tissue clay evaporates and is replaced with natural collagen.

Forehead Lift (Eyebrow Lift) From an incision behind the hairline, right across the top of the skull, deep creases in the forehead and frown lines can be eliminated as skin is adjusted upward. By removing portions of the muscles that create lines, the whole area is smoothed and tightened permanently, and the eyebrow itself is restored to a higher position. A brow lift may also accomplish much in the way of diminishing saggy lids. Folds of excess skin on the upper lids may merely be the result of a drooping browline. One caution: If a forehead lift is combined with excessive removal of upper eyelid skin, you may have trouble closing your eyes. If you are having your eyes done at the same time, the surgeon should perform the forehead lift first. Often when eyelid skin is smoothed this way, it eliminates the need for extensive eyelid surgery.

For Droopy Wrinkles, Sags, and Bags...

When skin loses its elasticity, anywhere on the face and neck, it begins to stretch and sag. Add deposits of fat to this redundant skin and upper eyelids may become hooded, lower eyelids may bag, and pouches may begin to proliferate along the jawline. Women, in particular, are prone to extra folds that form over the front part of the neck as muscles become lax.

Fat Evaporation Without tampering with the skin or muscle surrounding the eye, fatty pouches under the eye may be vaporized away. An electric needle-like probe heats the fat, steaming away 90 percent of it in two to three seconds. When the fat disappears, the pouches shrink instantly. With only a small incision made directly below the eyelash, swelling, bruising, and scarring is kept to a minimum, and healing time is accelerated. An optional way to remove this fat is transconjunctival blepharoplasty. A small incision is made inside the lower eyelid and the fat is surgically cut away. Stitches are often not necessary.

Blepharoplasty A traditional eye-lift may be in order if too much excess skin and fat accompanies sagging and pouching. Incisions are made in the natural lines and creases of either the upper or lower lids, or both, extending into the crow's feet at the corners. First the skin and muscle is separated from the underlying tissue, then excess fat, skin, and extra sagging muscle is removed.

Bone Sculpting The bony ridge just beneath the eyebrows can sometimes protrude too much, giv-ing eyes a hooded, heavy effect, even if the skin hasn't begun to sag. This bone (the supraorbital ridge) can be sculpted down to bring eyes out into the open.

Liposuction Often used in conjunction with a face-lift, liposuction sucks away the fat that causes puffiness at the chin and jowls. Although this procedure can be performed alone by inserting a hollow suctioning tube into the skin through a small incision under the chin, if done during a face-lift, it leaves no additional scars. This fat, which virtually contradicts youthful sculpting from chin to throat, may also be snipped away during face-lift surgery.

Full Face-Lift In the past five years, many surgeons have endorsed the extended "SMAS" procedure, which corrects facial structures that underlie the skin, including the muscle that wraps around the front of the throat and the area beneath the chin. The tight mask that resulted from simply stretching the skin taut is avoided, as the muscular layer responsible for the mobility and expression of the face (the Superficial Muscular Aponeurotic System) is elevated as well. From an incision inside the hairline at the temples, around the earlobe and into the nape of the neck in back, tissue is lifted, layer by layer, and excess skin is trimmed away as sagging muscles and connective tissues are tightened.

Growing Pains . . .

Gravity and collagen erosion can, over time, change the shape of features you've been comfortable with all your life. Your nose may lengthen and droop, descending beyond the ideal 100-to-105-degree angle. As the downward angle becomes more acute, it accentuates the hump of the bridge. Your earlobes may also appear longer. In fact, after the age of sixty or sixty-five, the ears actually start to grow again! If you've given the rest of your face a more youthful appearance, you may wish to consider redefining the tip of your nose with finesse sculpting rhinoplasty (a procedure that does not involve external cutting or breaking any bones in the nose). Tissue, as well as cartilage, muscle, and bone, is sculpted and molded from the inside. Earlobe reduction is another simple miniprocedure that can give the side view of your face an instant "lift"!

Consider Your Options

Planning a facial revision is not like picking one procedure from column A, one from column B. In many instances, less is more. You may not even need everything you're contemplating, and a good surgeon will tell you. On the other hand, it may make more sense to combine two or more procedures at the same time (nose and chin augmentation, for instance, or a face- and neck-lift). Certain combinations are extraordinarily helpful when done appropriately. In fact, if one part of your face becomes suddenly younger while another still bags and sags, the net effect may be more artificial than uplifting!

A reputable doctor will not suggest a shopping list of procedures. If your expectations overreach your anatomy, the doctor's wisest option is to tell you before you both begin. Disappointments can be costly to both doctor and patient. Similarly, a doctor can spot the occasional "plastisurgiholic," the patient who always wants to change this, and then that, and then that. Yet with more people having plastic surgery at an earlier age, multiple operations are becoming a fact of life. And it has nothing to do with the old myth that once you start, you have to keep at it. Today's procedures actually improve tone, build in support, and give you much more long-lasting results. A prudent doctor will dissuade a patient, however, if the condition of the skin and the patient's general health argues against prolonged anesthesia or healing time.

The Risk/Reward Ratio

No surgery is risk free. And that includes cosmetic surgery, even if it takes only ten minutes in a doctor's office. Make sure you know—exactly—what the complications might be for the procedure(s) you're considering. In addition to the most serious, although exceedingly rare, possibilities (facial nerve injury, blindness), there are other side effects that may trouble you. Ask your doctor about the chances of decrease in sensation or mobility, asymmetry, infection, abscess, hair loss, scarring, excess tearing, dry-eye syndrome, and blurred vision. Although most problems generally clear up by themselves, others may require a second procedure or even revisional surgery.

By being in the best possible physical condition before surgery, you will help to ward off major complications. Make sure you are well-rested, at a good body weight, and psychologically prepared for the surgery. Do not schedule surgery when you are going through a time of major trauma, stress, or depression. The immune system is intimately involved with the psychological aspects of distress, and you will heal in a very different way.

If you smoke, have your last cigarette one month before surgery; you don't want your blood vessels to be constricted. Without an oxygen-rich blood supply during surgery, especially during face-lift surgery, you could run the risk of actual skin death. Stop taking aspirin or Ibuprofin two to three weeks ahead; they inhibit clotting. Too much vitamin E does the same, and may encourage excessive bleeding. Extra nutritional supplements, however, can aid the healing process: Vitamin C maintains collagen and facilitates the formation of connective tis-

sue, plus it helps fight bacterial infections and prevents hemorrhaging. Trace minerals such as selenium, zinc, and manganese may preserve tissue elasticity, help heal wounds, and activate necessary enzymes. In general, a high-potency multi-vitamin is sufficient. And avoid crash dieting. Your body must not be in a protein-depleted state.

Just before surgery is the right time to do all hair coloring (the chemicals are an irritant and can't be used immediately after surgery), try a new hairstyle, or experiment with new cosmetics. Make sure you have no reaction to the products you're going to use while you heal. Change from contact lenses to glasses; no lenses may be worn the first week after eyelid surgery. And stay out of the sun. Skin inflammation is the last thing you need!

A little anxiety before your surgery is perfectly normal, but don't let it get the best of you. Channel it into excitement. Think positive thoughts. And set up a support system so that you'll be able to recuperate in a relaxed state. Have people around who will take care of you. The first few days, it's a must. After that, a little pampering will help chase away anesthesia-induced blues.

Plastic surgery *is* a big step, and there *are* risks. What about the rewards? Wait and see!

finishing touches

post-surgery
makeup

It's been said that good plastic surgery gets better with time; bad plastic surgery gets worse. In the first few days following your operation, you may fear the worst! There may be swelling, bruising, discoloration. Even the whites of your eyes may have turned bright red. Not to worry. You're in the process of healing. Your body is doing all it can to close the wound, exclude bacteria, and prevent fluid loss.

Although unsightly, swelling sends fluids into the area to get rid of toxins, literally "flushing out" the trauma of surgery. There *should* be swelling. Yet you want to keep it under control. Too much swelling can compress blood vessels and diminish blood supply to the tissue. So do what you can to minimize the accumulation of fluid. Sleep with the head of your bed elevated to drain fluids away. Apply cold compresses and ice packs if so instructed by your doctor.

"Settling" takes time. During the procedure, your skin tissues have been stretched and pulled; recuperative swelling stretches them a second time. But soon your skin's own elasticity will take over to "shrink" skin back to its normal size. Wound healing is also a very complex phenomenon. Just as bruising goes from bad to worse before it gets better, so does a scar. During the first three weeks, it might appear fairly flat and unobtrusive. Over the next few months, however, it may become your worst nightmare, often turning redder, thicker, and angry-looking. This should not be a cause for concern.

What's really going on behind the seams is the growth of new collagen, fibrous tissue, and blood vessels. There's a lot of activity at the incision site. The problem is, the process is random. New fibers don't know which way to go and so they tend to pile up, raising the scar. With simple finger massage, you can encourage the fibers to flatten and smooth out, which they should do within six weeks to six months after surgery. Some doctors advise using a light oil (vitamin E oil, for instance), and applying pressure in one direction along a scar. From approximately two to nine months, the scar is in its "remodeling" phase; it begins to flatten and lighten until it has reached its final cosmetic appearance. The whole healing process can take as long as two full years.

What you do during this time can influence the final outcome. Go into the sun without a block during the first three months, and you may end up with a much darker scar. Scars hold on to pig-

mentation longer than the surrounding skin—and any change in pigmentation could be permanent. In fact, scars that are not exposed to sunlight at all during the first year to year and a half tend to have better cosmetic results in the long run. So don't forget to use sunblock every day, winter, spring, summer, and fall!

Looking Better, Day by Day

While all of this change is going on, you can't very well run and hide. Although most bruising clears up in the first ten to fourteen days, areas of localized swelling may still be noticeable one month later. In fact, after nose reshaping, the tip may be more swollen than the bridge three months after surgery. It can take a good year for rhinoplasty to "settle;" a month and a half for results to be apparent from a face-lift or eyelid surgery. Be patient!

In the meantime, do all you can to look your best. Use makeup skillfully and carefully, and you'll enhance the wonderful new you you're in the process of becoming.

A Cosmetic Change Means a Change in Cosmetics

Eventually, if the planes and contours of your face have changed, you'll need to rethink makeup placement. But that's down the road. When you're ready, I suggest you have a professional makeup consultation. You need someone to convince you that your "new" face is really you! Many women feel safer resorting to tried-and-true techniques, but this is a huge mistake. You've begun an exciting new adventure; see it through.

What you'll most be concerned with is getting through the first six weeks, then the first six months, when your transformation may be just a bit startling. Resist the temptation to hide under a heavy mask of makeup; this will only draw attention to the problems you want to camouflage most, especially if you're a woman who has always worn a very natural makeup—it's a dead giveaway. Instead, a light hand and a little skill will do more to create an attractive appearance.

Three Steps to Perfect Post-Op Makeup

Let your makeup progress with the healing process. You may find that you have to concentrate on one area of your face at one time, another at another time. In general, I recommend a three-step strategy for early, mid, and late healing periods. Here's the timetable:

Weeks 1–2: No Makeup at All

Let the stitches come out and give the incision a chance to heal. Although it seals in twelve to twenty-four hours, a stitch line is not strong. Stretching and pulling your face to apply makeup may cause it to re-open. Makeup is also not sterile—never apply

it to an open wound. Because all tissues heal differently, you may be able to gently apply makeup earlier, but always ask your surgeon.

Weeks 2–4: Early Makeup

Address bruising and discoloration.

Weeks 5–12: Mid Makeup

Begin to camouflage swelling and incisions.

Months 3–6: Late Makeup

Deal with scarring. This is just when they suddenly act up.

On the next few pages, you'll see how this strategy may be applied to three of the most common procedures: nose reshaping, eyelid surgery, and face-lifts. These tips should get you out the door and back into circulation if you spend a little time practicing them. Don't panic and try to desperately "hide" something five minutes before you have to go out. Your last-minute efforts are only going to emphasize it!

The Nose
A Natural New Look

There may be a dressing on your nose and packing inside it immediately following the surgery. Even after everything has been removed, there may be generalized swelling around the nose, under the eyes, and from the ridge of the cheekbone to the laugh lines. There is often bruising around the eyes, which disappears in about three weeks or less.

Early Makeup Use a creamy camouflage preparation to cover the bruises. Although I do not endorse products, I will name names here because certain products have been developed specifically for use after surgery and are more effective than standard cosmetic concealers. You should know what to ask for. Lydia O'Leary's Covermark products and Dermablend are two of the best. They're more opaque than foundations, yet creamy enough to slide on easily. Because they are heavier, apply them under your foundation. Then *dab* foundation—your normal shade—over the area, for greater coverage (1). Don't rub it in, or you'll remove some of your camouflage cover in the process. Keep makeup light and uncomplicated at this point; you don't want to draw too much attention to your face just yet. Add a light touch of powder, a natural lipstick, and that's it.

Mid Makeup As the swelling redistributes, balance your face with blush. If your cheek area is swollen, place blush on the outside of the cheeks. Don't try to "contour" hollows with dark blusher now; it will be all too obvious. Direct the eye away from, rather than toward, the swelling. Continue to keep makeup minimal, but add touches of color: mascara on lashes, blush on brow bone, a fresh, clear-color lipstick that's not too light or too bright.

Late Makeup

When swelling drops to the bottom half of your nose, your face can look suddenly out of proportion. Now is the time to try new balancing techniques. Widen the distance between your brows to soften the central focus on the nose. Place your lipstick slightly inside the natural line of your upper lip to draw attention downward. And use two colors of lipstick, in the same family: a lighter shade on top, a deeper one below. Never apply blush lower on your cheek than where the nostrils begin to flare, keeping it well away from the nose. If the contrast between the bridge of your nose and the tip requires greater sculpting ingenuity to bring everything into balance, highlight along each side with concealer or a lighter shade of base. Remember, if you use concealer, dab it on *top* of your base, then powder to integrate it and blot.

3

The Eyes
Go Easy, Go Slowly

Thin eyelid skin bruises very easily, so you may have two very nice "shiners" after surgery. The discoloration will fade quickly, but in the process, your skin may turn every shade of the rainbow!

Early Makeup Gently apply camouflage cream with a small cotton swab or sable eyeliner brush to bruised areas only; don't go near the incisions. With under-eye swelling a very common occurrence for a while, it's going to look as if your bags haven't packed up and left! Don't accentuate them with a concealer that borders on white. Instead, use a foundation just a half tone lighter than your normal base and dab it on the area with a latex sponge. Dipped in water first, a sponge liquifies bases to a very light consistency, the weight you want for delicate skin. No need to apply blush right now—there's enough of a color show going on! Skip eyeliner, eye shadow, or mascara during this initial period as well.

When your bruises begin to turn from blue to red to yellowish-green, adjust your foundation accordingly with under-bases (most good cosmetic lines include them). First, begin with a yellow-based foundation shade to neutralize blue skin. Add a green under-base when it begins to turn red; a lavender under-base when it evolves into yellow. If this stage of bruising isn't all that obvious, simply use a regular foundation with a bit of a pink tint for a rosy glow.

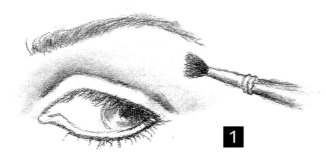

Mid Makeup If you want to deal with your incisions now, it's fine. But use foundation rather than concealer or camouflage creams, which tend to ridge up in lid creases. Adjust any residual swelling with colored shadows. But never go near your eyes with an applicator! Use the softest brushes you can buy (1). They may not apply the product as well, but they also don't stretch the skin. You can use eyeliner now, but stay away from pencils that you have to drag across the lid. Dip a moistened brush into a powder eye shadow to line (2). Choose a mascara that is water soluble, without fibers; you must be able to remove it easily without rub-

bing a tissue or remover pad across your lids (3). Preferably, your mascara will splash off easily and you can pat your eyes dry gently. When it comes to blush, don't apply it too high on the cheekbones. It will look like you haven't lost your redness yet!

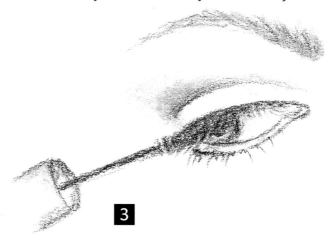

Late Makeup Swelling and discoloration should have cleared up by now. But this is when the scars come out to play. You may have a hint of a scar in the crease of the upper lid; in the lower lid it will have virtually disappeared. You may first want to smooth the entire upper lid area with an eyelid primer in a natural shade (no white, please). Then sculpt and define your beautiful new eyelid crease with a soft, smoky matte color placed just above it, a lighter shade from crease to lash. Add a highlight of blush just above the darker shadow. When you line your upper lid, extend the line slightly upward, as a continuation of the last lash. This draws the attention away from any tiny scar in the crow's feet area.

The Face-Lift

Facing Up to New Contours

While the healing for a face-lift is the most complex, it is the easiest procedure of all to camouflage, especially for women—the scars are hidden around the ears and in the hairline.

Early Makeup Your face may rival the color display of the northern lights, with discoloration reaching from temples to the base of your neck. Don't despair. Use your camouflage cream before applying base. Then dab, don't smudge, a matte base over it. Use the progression of under-bases described in the Eye section, above, to keep up with bruises as they turn from blue to red to yellow. Behind your ear, use a compact powder, not a foundation, over the camouflage cream; liquid foundations always tend to ride up into the hair. Avoid blush altogether during this period. You have enough color to contend with!

Mid Makeup Discoloration has essentially disappeared, but swelling and incision lines are still obvious. Use blush and color accents placed away from the center of the face. If you want to sculpt your face a bit to give it a thinner appearance, use a brown-based foundation from mid-ear, blending and lightening toward the middle of the cheek. You can accentuate the jawline a little with the same shade, but keep it subtle. Always powder over to unify. Pretty scarves at the neck or high necklines can draw attention away from around-the-ear incisions. Keep your hair loose and full at the jawline—no ponytails or up-swept dos now!

Late Makeup The focus can return to the center of your face now. Play up the eyes and the lips for all they're worth. The scar behind your earlobe to your hairline will become particularly tricky at this point. It stays noticeable the longest and is the most obvious. To minimize it, don't just cover the entire area behind your ear with concealer. Use a cotton swab dipped in camouflage cream and apply it carefully along the scar line. And always press a matte compact powder over the concealer; shine attracts light and accentuates the scar. If a scar is still apparent in front of your ear, use the camouflage followed by your normal (matte) foundation in the same shade as the compact powder. Fix immediately with loose powder. Without it, the heat of your skin makes the thicker camouflage cream slide right off, taking all your cover with it!

With every procedure, after six months, you're on your own. Balance and harmony will have returned to your facial structure and skin tone. Will it have been worth it? For that matter, are any of the techniques included in this book really worth it once a woman reaches "a certain age"? Only you can decide. But I emphatically believe that they *are* justified if they keep you liking the woman who stares back at you in the mirror. I wish you love.